T0208832

PREVIOUS BOOKS

Spiritual Wisdom for Peace on Earth From Sananda
Channeled through David J Adams

LOVE is the **KEY.** Part 1
Spiritual Wisdom from Germain
Channeled through David J Adams

LOVE is the **KEY.** Part 2
Spiritual Wisdom from Germain
Channeled through David J Adams

WE ARE ALL ONE

Spiritual Wisdom from
The Masters of Shambhala

Channeled Through
David J Adams

authorHOUSE®

AuthorHouse™
1663 Liberty Drive
Bloomington, IN 47403
www.authorhouse.com
Phone: 1 (800) 839-8640

Published by AuthorHouse 02/22/2019

ISBN: 978-1-7283-0081-8 (sc)
ISBN: 978-1-7283-0079-5 (hc)
ISBN: 978-1-7283-0080-1 (e)

Library of Congress Control Number: 2019901958

The Front Cover Sacred Geometry is called the 'Labyrinth of Inner Vision'.

The Labyrinth was painted by and photographed by Kaye Ogilvie, Intuitive artist from Queensland, Australia based on a concept channeled through David J Adams.

Back Cover Photo was taken on the camera of David J Adams, the T shirt was created by Tie Dye artist, Ruth Cary Cooper from USA.

Print information available on the last page.

DEDICATION

I Dedicate this book to my children, Nicky and Suzi, my grandchildren, Lauren, Matthew and Emily, and my great grandchildren, Ruby–Rae and Peyton, for they and others of the next generations will carry the Light forward and create the Peace that we all yearn for.

ABOUT THE AUTHOR

ADAMS, David John Patrick

Born: 28th April 1943

At: Mountain Ash, Glamorgan, South Wales, UK.

Moved to South Australia in 1971, Currently living in the southern suburbs of the city of Adelaide.

Began his Spiritual Journey as a result of the Harmonic Convergence in late 1987.

In 1991, he was asked by Beloved Master Germain to undertake a global Meditation based on, and working with, the Consciousness of the Oceans, which was called the Marine Meditation.

In 2009 he was asked to address a Peace Conference in Istanbul to speak of the Marine Meditation and his work for World Peace through meditation.

He is a Songwriter, a Musician, an Author and Channel, but most of all a **SERVANT OF PEACE**.

David began bringing through information from a variety of Masters and Cosmic Beings in the form of Meditations around 1991. It was not, however, until after the year 2000 that he began to channel messages in group situations and in individual sessions. Most of these messages were not recorded or transcribed so remain shared with only a few people, but in 2009 the messages being brought through in the weekly Pendragon Meditation group began to be recorded and transcribed by Kath Smith and sent out around the world on David's own Pendragon network.

David's special Guide and Mentor has been 'The Germain, the I am that I am', but he has also worked extensively with – and channeled - Sananda, Hilarion, Djwahl Khul, AA Michael, The Merlin, The Masters of Shambhala, as well as Arcturian Sound Master Tarak and his own Home Trinity Cosmic Brother Ar'Ak.

(Contact email – <u>djpadams8@tpg.com.au</u>)

ACKNOWLEDGEMENTS

I, David J Adams, would like to acknowledge three special Earth Angels.

Heather Niland/Shekina Shar - who helped me to awaken to my Journey in 1987 and connected me to my Beloved Friend "The Germain", she was a mentor, guide and teacher way ahead of her time.

Meredith Pope – who walked in the same shoes as me in those difficult early years as a fellow 'weekender' at The EarthMother Centre, and was - and still is - an inspiration to me.

Krista Sonnen – An Harmonic and Earthwalker, who helped to build the bridges to my Spiritual and Cosmic friends by persistently urging me to allow them to speak through me in private sessions, then in group sessions. Without her support these messages would not be here.

I would further like to acknowledge **Kath Smith** – A spiritual Being of immense Love and Joy who initiated the recording and transcribing of the messages received in Pendragon so that the messages from our 'other Dimensional friends' would not be lost forever. Also **Takara Shelor,** who combined her Global Water Dolphin Meditation with the Marine Meditation in 1998 and has organized the Marine Meditation website as an adjunct to her own Dolphin Empowerment website ever since. Also **Kaye Ogilvie**, Intuitive Spiritual Artist, who Painted all the Labyrinths walked during the Marine Meditations, as well as many other inspirational images that have assisted my Journey of Growth.

I also acknowledge all those here in Australia and those throughout the World who have supported me and encouraged me over the years, and in particular, **Barbara Wolf and Margaret Anderson**, who's vision and hard work has made this book possible.

BLESSINGS OF LOVE, JOY AND PEACE TO EACH AND EVERY ONE OF YOU.

DAVID J ADAMS

FOREWORD

We Humans live in the concept of "Linear Time', which divides 'Time' into minutes, hours, days, months, etc. and goes in a straight line from 'Past' through 'Present' to 'Future', consequently we give importance to the date on which something happens. Our Spiritual and Cosmic Friends are not bound by such constraints, they operate in the **'Now'** moment, so although the messages within this book have 'dates' attached to them, they are, essentially, **TIMELESS**.

Some messages do, of course, refer to specific events, such as the Equinox or the Solstice, or even some man made event, however, the underlying message is always **TIMELESS**. So we ask, when you read these messages, that you accept them as having importance within the **'Now Moment'** of your lives. Although we have given the date of receipt at the end of each message, they are not in sequential 'linear time' order.

All messages were received within the Pendragon Meditation Circle and always began with the 'Sounding" of the Tibetan Bowls, the Blessings Chimes, the Drum, and occasionally other percussion instruments. Many of the messages make reference to these Sound frequencies.

Let the messages speak to your Heart, for that is what they were intended to do when they were given by the **Masters of Shambhala**.

Blessings of Love, Peace and Joy

David J Adams

INTRODUCTION

From Time to Time, all Ascended Masters, Archangels, Cosmic Ambassadors and Light Beings of many Dimensions gather together in **'Council'** or **'Congress'** to work out how best they can assist Earth Mother (sometimes referred to as **Gaia**) in the development, or **'Ascension'** of the Earth Planet itself. Nothing is **'imposed'** upon the Earth, everything is by **'mutual agreement'**. This gathering invariably takes place at **Shambhala** – a 'Light City' in a higher Dimensional Frequency.

Although I had been channeling individual Ascended Masters and Cosmic Ambassadors for many years, it was not until February 2012 that I received my first communication directly from one of these gatherings, under the **'ONENESS'** name of **'The Masters of Shambhala'**. Within the channelings many different voices spoke at different times, so it was a unique energy experience for me and one for which I will be eternally grateful.

I am delighted to have the opportunity to share the Words of Wisdom from **the Masters of Shambhala** in this book. I hope you will find them uplifting and inspiring,

Blessings of Love, Peace and Joy.

David J Adams

(djpadams8@tpg.com.au)

CONTENTS

1

DISCERNMENT, DISCERNMENT, DISCERNMENT

(The Circle opens with the Sounds of the Tibetan Bowls and the Blessings Chimes)

Greetings Dear Hearts, we are the Masters of Shambhala.

Discernment, Discernment, Discernment - If we could etch that one word in your sky, that each morning as you leave your homes you look and you see that word, we would do so, because it is of pivotal importance at this time - this time of great change. For often times when change occurs there comes confusion, and you do not know what to embrace, and what to let go of.

Since you are still in your 'Olympic period', perhaps we can give a sporting analogy to indicate what we mean by discernment - Imagine yourself as a team, perhaps we should call it "The Light Workers Team" racing towards the finish line called "Ascension", and along your route there is a crowd on each side, a crowd of family, of friends, of supporters, and many others you do not necessarily know. Each one calls out their encouragement, their advice, to each and every one of you. It becomes a wall of sound assailing you, a plethora of pearls of wisdom flowing around you, flowing over you, flowing through you, and you wonder which one of these to pluck from the ethers, which one will enhance your journey, which one is right.

There is confusion, for the advice that is being given may not be for you, it may be for someone else in your team that is racing beside you, or behind you, or in front of you, for words of wisdom for an initiate who is just beginning are no longer words of wisdom for someone half ways down the track, or someone approaching their Mastery.

You need to reach deep within your Hearts and ask for guidance from within, for only you - within your Heart - knows where you are on your journey.

Only you know what you need to enhance your journey.

Only your Heart has the discernment to separate the wheat from the chaff and to embrace only that which is for you, to separate that from all the hubbub of noise and take it into your Heart - *discernment Dear Ones - discernment.*

There will of course be those in the crowd who are not of family, or friends, or supporters. They are there purposely to slow you down, to trip you up, to give you advice which seems on the surface to be positive, but is designed to take away your own power - and only your Heart can discern what is good for you, and what is not.

You need to have total confidence in yourself.

You are all powerful Beings of Light.

Embrace your own power, accept the encouragement of your friends and families, but move within your Hearts and exercise the discernment that is necessary to move forward clearly, purposefully to your own Ascension. When you stay true to your own Heart, you are gifting assistance and Light to all the other members of your team. They too must operate discernment for themselves.

You cannot carry them, you can only share your Light and your Wisdom, and allow them to choose through their discernment what they wish to take on board.

Discernment – place that word within your Hearts, feel it, breathe it, act upon it, for if you do not, you will surrender your power once more, and in surrendering your power you begin to fall back, and the finishing line of Ascension gets further and further away.

Discernment is the key in these times of great change and confusion, and only your Heart can provide that discernment for you.

We thank you for allowing us to share this message with you tonight, and we bless each and every one of you.

(6th August 2012)

2

SHARE THE ENERGY OF 'KINDNESS'

(The Circle opens with the Sounds of the Tibetan bowls and the Indigenous clap sticks)

Embrace the vibrations of Sound as waves of Love flowing through every aspect of your Being. Feel the Light within your Hearts growing brighter and brighter, spreading out across the Earth with each beat of your Heart, empowering the Awakening of all upon the Earth at this time, allowing each and every Being to see their personal journeys in the Light of the *WHOLE*.

Greetings, Dear Hearts, we are the Masters of Shambhala.

We have come to you tonight to speak to you of *'Kindness'*, a simple word, a simple term that each of you will perceive slightly differently, but in this time of great change upon your Planet it is easy to see dark clouds - as chaos shows it's self in various places - and it is important to create the necessary balance by invoking from deep within your Hearts the energies of *'Kindness'*.

You begin by being kind to yourself ! many of your Spirit friends have spoken to you before about Loving yourselves, and Kindness is a part of that Loving. It is about accepting yourself, not judging yourself. It is about lifting yourself up when you perceive that you have fallen down, when your actions are less - perhaps in your perceptions - than Loving.

It is important to embrace yourself with the energies of 'Kindness', for as with Love itself you cannot be kind to other people unless you allow yourself to be kind to yourself, to be totally accepting of yourself.

It is not easy for Humanity to let go of judgment, and the primary judgment you make is about yourself, so, Dear Hearts, embrace yourself with the energy of Kindness, for Kindness accepts frailty - perceived or real. It accepts you as you are, and it embraces you and uplifts you. *If you embrace yourself with Kindness you bring a smile to your own face, and by so doing you spread that smile to others.*

From time to time there have been modest movements on your Planet to embrace the concept of *'Kindness'*, gifting Kindness to others, but like many of Human fads, it quickly fades and you return to judgment of yourself, of others, and those *'random acts of Kindness'* disappear. We at Shambhala are asking you now to focus more each day, each and every minute of each day, on extending those random acts of Kindness into *purposeful acts of Kindness, deliberate acts of Kindness*.

Share the energy of *'Kindness'* with all those that you meet. Do not judge first, do not look at others and think "Ahh they are in need of my Kindness". That is a judgment ! simply surround them with the energy of Kindness from within your Heart. Embrace them with the energy of Kindness.

You see, as with Love, Dear Hearts, *'Kindness' is an energy, it is not merely an action, it is not merely an expression – it is a beautiful, Loving energy,* and you are quite capable of sharing that energy with all those you meet, irrespective of your judgments of them, and this, Dear Hearts, is what is needed on your Planet at this time, it needs for people, for Humans, to come together and embrace each other with the energy of *'Kindness'*.

'Kindness' is both a giving and a receiving.
   It is not a payment for something given to you.
      It is simply an exchange of *Loving Energies*.

As you come together in groups it is important to share the energies of *'Kindness',* and through those *'Energies of Kindness exchanges'* more and more Light, and more and more Love will be created upon the Earth, and as this happens, there will be less and less judgment, for in *'Kindness'* you accept the equality of others.

But first, and most importantly. be kind to yourselves!

Everything begins within your Heart - the Love, the Light and the Kindness begins in your Heart, and it surrounds YOU first, before moving outwards to embrace all others.

So do not speak from now on about *'random acts of Kindness'*, speak simply about *permanently* sharing the energies of *'Kindness'* from within your Heart.

We bless you Dear Hearts.

(24ᵗʰ June 2013)

3

PEACE ON EARTH IS NOT A CONCEPT, IT IS A REALITY WITHIN THE HEARTS OF EVERY BEING

(The Circle opens with the Sounds of the Tibetan bowls, the Blessings Chimes and the Thunder stick.)

Embrace the Peace deep within your Heart. Empower that Peace with your will and your intent and then radiate that Peace forth out across the Earth, connecting the Peace within your Heart to the Peace within the Hearts of all of Humanity, and as you do so feel the Oneness of Peace on Earth, for *Peace on Earth is not a concept, it is a reality within the Hearts of every Being,* and as you breathe, breathe in the Blue Mist of Peace, and as you breathe out, breathe out the Blue Light of Peace, empowered by your Heart, and imagine that Blue Light of Peace spreading across the Earth.

Imagine every Being of Light upon the Earth Planet breathing in the Blue Mist of Peace, and breathing out the Blue Light of Peace, for in your Human minds the word 'mist' implies a certain concealment, but Light is something clear and bright, so breathe in the Mist, the Blue Mist of Peace and radiate forth the Blue Light of Peace, for you, Dear Hearts, are the *'transformers'*, you draw in one energy and you radiate forth a new enhanced energy, enhanced by the Divine Love you have for yourself and for everyone upon the Earth.

Greetings, Dear Hearts, we are The Masters of Shambhala.

We embrace you with deepest Love, we embrace you with the powerful energies of Peace, and we invite each and every one of you to activate the Joy within yourself as you transmute the Blue Mist of Peace into the Blue Light of Peace - change that which is hidden from Humanity into that which enlightens Humanity - each of the energies are vibrant Peace, as each is a variation of the 'theme' of Peace.

As you know, Dear Hearts, the Sacred Isle of Avalon was hidden by the mist for eons of time, to preserve the essence of Peace that existed in that special place, that special Dimensional Frequency of Love, Peace and Joy, but now it is time to draw that Mist into your Heart and transmute it, and allow the Sacred Isle of Avalon to once again become visible to the Hearts of all Humanity, for you see, Dear Hearts, Avalon was never for the minds of Humanity, it was always for the Hearts of Humanity and when Humans moved from Heart based living into mind based living they lost their connection to the Sacred energies of Avalon, but now the time is right to reawaken the seeds of Peace and Love and Joy within every Being upon your Planet, that within those Hearts may rise again the Sacred Isle of Avalon.

Your mythology, Dear Hearts, personifies Avalon as the Divine Feminine, perceives it as the priestesses, the reality, Dear Hearts, is that *Avalon exists only within the Heart* and it is the Heart itself which is perceived as the Divine Feminine, the essence of compassion, of feeling, of Love, all those energies that have been set aside in your patriarchal societies which rely upon the logic of the mind.

Dear Hearts, logic will still exist in the future, but not as a dominant force, but as a servant of the Heart.

The energies of Peace are flowing powerfully onto the Earth Planet. The new Song of the Earth - the new vibrational frequencies of Sound - will absorb greater and greater levels of Peace, always through your Hearts.

You may have noticed, Dear Hearts, that in recent years the focus of this Circle has been the Heart, ***everything begins, everything grows, everything expands within the Heart.*** The images of the Heart are powerful symbols, but this is the time to move beyond the symbolic and accept the reality that the Heart is everything, infinite Love, Divine Peace, the ecstasy of Joy, all these are incorporated within your Heart, all these have been hidden within you for eons of time on your Earth Planet - The times of separation and of darkness - but through the work that you and we have done together, the new frequencies of the Earth accept and acknowledge this new enlightenment.

So once more, Dear Hearts, we ask you to breathe in the Blue Mist of Peace and breathe out the Blue Light of Peace. Accept that this is why you are here on the Earth Planet at this time, to *BE* the transducers of the forgotten energy of Peace, turning it into a reality of life for you, within you, and radiating from you.

You will find, Dear Hearts, as you reach out in Peace you will receive that same Peace and Love from others, other Humans, other animals. You will sense a change in vibration in your surroundings, for as you well know, Dear Hearts, 'like attracts like' and *you will become a magnet for Peace*.

We embrace you, Dear Hearts, with deepest Love and we thank you for all the work that you have done to this time to bring enlightenment into your Hearts, and through your Hearts bring enlightenment to the Earth Planet.

(27th October 2014)

4

THE NEW EARTH IS HEART BASED

(The Circle opens with the Sounds of the Tibetan bowls and the Blessings Chimes)

Embrace the Peace within your Heart and allow that energy of Peace to be breathed out into the world, to create a vibrational frequency that uplifts the Souls of all who walk the Earth Planet at this time.

The energy of Peace is the foundation stone of the new Earth, and Peace comes from the Divine Love that your Soul brings to your physical Being, for this is a time for each and every one of you to acknowledge the blessedness of yourself and to gift that blessedness to all those around you, freely, unconditionally.

Greetings, Dear Hearts, we are the Masters of Shambhala,

We have come together once again to embrace each and every one of you with the energy of Divine Love, with the energy of Peace.

As Humans in a third dimensional world you rely almost exclusively upon the guidance of your minds, and your minds need to be able to picture what is to come, and yet, Dear Hearts, at this particular juncture in your time it is important not to start projecting from your minds to create the future of your Planet, for your minds still hold the energies of the old Earth, the memories of the old Earth, and if you project from your mind to create anew on the new Earth you will simply be repeating the shadows of the old.

It is imperative to simply *BE* within your Heart at this time and to allow the energies within your Heart - the energies of Divine Love and the energies of Peace - to simply *BE,* and to sit and watch as those energies begin to create a new Earth for you, an Earth not based on material objects, an Earth based on energies, and what more beautiful energies could there be than Divine Love and Divine Peace?

At your last gathering Beloved Djwahl Khul spoke of 'breath and breathing' and we come tonight to reinforce that message, and we ask you to breathe out into the world the energies that exist within your Hearts. You do not need to put those energies into any form, those are constructs of the old mind, the new Earth needs to be built on the foundations of energy - *the energy of Love - the energy of Peace,* and if you breathe forth those energies from within your Heart and allow those energies to permeate every aspect of the Earth, the structures that your minds enjoy so much will begin to create themselves from Higher Dimensional Frequencies, from your Soul Self.

The new Earth needs to begin afresh the way the old Earth began, with energies - not with form or matter - but with energies, and this time the energies will be molded by your Souls. So let your minds take a rest, allow them to function on a level that simply meets your needs for the moment, but allow the greater creativity that is necessary to formulate the new Earth to come from your Heart and from your Soul, for *the Heart and the Soul together will create a magical world where Love and Peace are not contaminated by the egos of Humanity.*

We recognize, Dear Hearts, that it is difficult for Humans to turn off their minds, but it is necessary, for the new Earth is Heart based and the mind will gradually learn to accept and acknowledge the guidance of the Heart and the guidance of the Soul.

The new Earth is new energy, form and matter will follow in new Light frequencies, but they need to be constructed from your Heart, so over the next few weeks or months in your time scales sit within your Hearts and simply empower the energies of Divine Love and Divine Peace and breathe them out into the world, and give them the freedom to create the new Earth without mental expectations of how this should be, of how this should look, of how this should feel.

*It is time to honour your Heart, to embrace your Soul, and simply to **BE** within the Light frequencies of Love and Peace.*

(26th October 2015)

5

HEAVEN IS NOT REMOTE – HEAVEN LIES WITHIN YOU

(The Circle opens with the Tibetan Bowls and the Blessings Chimes)

The Blessings Chimes Sound for everyone in need of healing at this time, anyone in need of uplifting in Spirit, and the Tibetan Bowls call to the Joy within your Hearts to also be uplifted into the reality of your day to day lives. For it is so easy upon the Earth Planet to become dismayed, disappointed and disillusioned as you walk the pathway of your lives, but once you move inside and embrace the Joy within your Hearts, you change your own perspective on life, and by so doing you re - create the journey that you are on.

Greetings, Dear Hearts, we are the Masters of Shambhala, and we come to you tonight with an urgent message of the necessity for perceiving Joy at all times within your lives, for *Joy is the Heart beat of the Earth Planet,* and when you embrace the Joy within your own Heart you become One with the Earth Planet and together you are uplifted into new frequencies of Light and Sound, you begin to create the Heaven on Earth that is spoken of so much on you Planet.

'Heaven' is not remote, it is not something out beyond your Planet – *HEAVEN LIES WITHIN YOU,* it needs to be released from within you in order to manifest itself upon the Earth Planet. For too long, Dear Hearts, you have looked upon Heaven as being remote from you, when all the time it has been within you waiting to be birthed into reality in your life.

We have spoken to you many times about Oneness, about all of us being part of the Whole and yet much of Humanity continues to perceive Heaven as being somewhere out there in the Universe, some creation that is not you, but we are here to tell you, Dear Hearts, Heaven IS within you, and to create Heaven on Earth is simply to allow that Heaven within you to emerge, to emerge in the way you treat yourself, in the way you treat others. You find the Joy within your Hearts, you find the Love within your Hearts and you find Respect within your Hearts, and when you bring these things out into your world you create a different Dimension.

Perception and perspective are so important, reach within yourselves, ***KNOW with great certainty that within YOU lies the Heaven that you seek.***

Last week, Dear Hearts, beloved Germain spoke to you of 'faith', giving you a totally different perspective on that word, and tonight we do the same for the word 'Heaven', for once more the word Heaven has been taken up in your religious beliefs and a vision of that Heaven has been created external to you, but the reality is, it exists within YOU at all times.

When you have faith in yourself you are free to move into yourself and uncover and discover the essence of Heaven. Heaven is the highest vibrational frequency of YOU. Each one of you will feel Heaven differently, will perceive Heaven differently for it exists within you, it is a vibration, high frequency vibration, that creates the essence of 'feeling', of Love, of Joy, excitement, bliss, ecstasy, all these things come from the Heaven within you. *They do not create the Heaven for you, they come from the Heaven within you.*

In bringing this to your attention, Dear Hearts, we are not separating you from all the rest of Humanity, we are simply inviting you to share the Real You with the rest of Humanity, to allow others to feel the Heaven that is within you.

We hope, Dear Hearts, that you will begin to find the Heaven within you, and share the energy of that Heaven with all those around you, for all the goodness that is within you comes from the highest frequencies of Light - *AND THAT IS HEAVEN.*

Enjoy opening and embracing the Heaven within you.

(13th April 2015)

6

THE WATERS OF THE WORLD ARE CALLING OUT FOR LOVE FREQUENCIES

(The Circle opens with the Sound of the Tibetan Bowl and the Drum)

Greetings, Dear Hearts. we are the Masters of Shambhala

As you are aware the Earth Planet is going through much change, and many different Cosmic energies have poured into the Planet over recent times to assist with these changes. Many of you have noticed that the physical vessels you inhabit in this incarnation have not always been able to accept, embrace and balance these energies, as a result, existing imbalances within that body have been amplified and perhaps even new imbalances have appeared. This is quite normal and natural when high frequency energies have to react with the dense mass of your Dimensional frequency, but you will need to work upon yourselves to restore the balance and harmony of your bodies.

Just as you Humans have had difficulties accepting, embracing and balancing these Cosmic energies, so too has the Earth Planet itself, which is of course also in part a dense mass within the third Dimension.

We have come today to ask for your assistance in alleviating these difficulties within the Earth Planet. As you know, the majority of the surface of the Earth Planet is covered in water, and it is therefore within the world of water that the necessary adjustments need to be made.

The Waters of the World are not in the Pristine condition that they were originally, pollution has contaminated the Water in many parts of the World, partially as a result of Human activities and partially as a result of the Earth itself through volcanic eruptions. This is why the Waters of the World are having difficulty also accepting, embracing and balancing these Cosmic energies

As you are aware, there is a symbiotic relationship, energetically and spiritually, between the Waters of the World and the moon, so alleviating and balancing the new Cosmic High Frequency energies need for BOTH to be worked with. We are therefore here to ask you to participate with us *"in ceremony"* for the period of ONE Moon cycle.

We suggest that you place within a glass bowl one or more shells from the Ocean to represent the Waters of the World, and one or more Moonstone crystals to represent the Lunar energies, then cover these with water. It can be Ocean, lake, river, spring or creek water, whatever feels right to you. We further suggest that you commence the ceremony at the time of the next Full moon by placing the bowl outside to embrace the Lunar energies, then the next day bring the bowl back inside and place it in a Sacred Space within your home where you can work and play with it for the duration of the Lunar Cycle, then at the next full moon, again place the bowl outside to embrace the Lunar energies.

When that ceremony has been completed the water within the bowl will have been infused with dynamic energies of balance and Harmony, and we suggest that you place a little of the water back into the Ocean, lake, river, spring or creek from whence it came, then use the remainder as a personal crystal/ shell/lunar elixir, for don't forget that the physical vessels you enjoy within the Earth Dimension are also mainly water.

For many years you have worked with your Marine Meditation to inform others that *the Oceans have a 'Consciousness'*, and that *where there is a Consciousness there is the capability of 'communication'*. Beloved Dr Emoto, who now sits with us at Shambhala, also set out to educate people of the Consciousness that Water possesses, with his many experiments on how water reacts and responds to the stimulus of Songs, Sound and words – spoken or written.

You thought perhaps that your time of working with the Oceans was at an end, but that is not so, we are asking you once again to move into your Hearts and communicate with the Consciousness of the Waters of the World so that both of you together can mutually assist one another to more readily accept, embrace and balance the new High Frequencies of Light.

Dear Hearts, please do not perform this ceremony with solemnity, the essence of the new Light frequencies is "Joy", so you need to embrace the ceremony with Joy in your Hearts. This is not 'Devotion', this is Delight !. Do not be afraid to ***"Play"*** with the bowl containing the Shells and the crystals, perhaps surrounding them with different crystals all the time or different colours, or even placing written messages on the bowl itself and beneath it, inviting the Waters of the World to work with the moon energies to create a new joyful energy within the Oceans and the lakes and the rivers and the creeks. Words such as ***"Love", "Joy", "Peace", "Harmony",*** even ***"Laughter"*** will all help to create the desired effect.

Of course, Dear Hearts, these are only suggestions, you live in a world of Free Will, so you can make your own choices of how you perform the ceremony and even when you do so, but of course we will hope that you will choose to work with us from the next full Moon to the full moon afterwards. Whatever you decide to do must ***'Feel'*** right within your own Hearts.

The Waters of the World are calling out for Love frequencies to assist them at this time, so let us all

Play together for a Lunar Cycle, we are sure that it will be of great help to Earth Mother.

We thank you and bless you.

(8TH July 2016)

7

THIS IS THE TIME OF RESURRECTION FOR THE WHOLE OF THE EARTH

(The Circle opens with the Sounds of the Tibetan Bowls, the drum and the Blessings Chimes.)

As the vibrations of Sound radiate through your Being, feel them loosen any last remaining shadows from the past, filling your Being with *pure Sound, pure Light, pure Love,* and feel yourselves being released from the tentacles of darkness from the past, and feel your Heart begin to pulse with a Love far greater than you have ever experienced before.

Greetings, Dear Hearts, we are The Masters of Shambhala.

We have come together once more to prepare the way, to prepare the waves of energy that will permeate your Planet at the time of the Equinox, for this is a time of great significance for the Earth Planet, it will be a significant change in direction for the whole of the Earth as you emerge into a new Dimensional Frequency of Light, one that has no place in duality, separation and density. It is a Light that speaks of freedom, freedom within the *Oneness of all that is*.

All your friends are together with us at this time sitting in Council, not in judgment. It is important to remember that, Dear Hearts, we sit in Council, not in judgment of you, of the Earth, of all that has happened in the past, for this is the time of resurrection for the whole of the Earth, and all the Masters who for eons of time have given of themselves to assist in the Ascension of the Earth Planet, have all come back from their various journeys through the Cosmos to be at this place, at this time, such, Dear Hearts. is the significance of this particular Equinox.

It is the Equinox of Unity and you will feel the power of the waves of Oneness that will flow through the whole of the Earth Planet, that will activate aspects of your Heart, aspects of your brain, aspects of your Soul that have been dormant since you chose to enter the realm of duality.

That is now gone, Dear Heart, it is only the illusion that remains. It is a time for looking deep within your Hearts and rediscovering the Oneness within you.

Shambhala is filled with Masters of Sound, Masters of Light, Masters of Love from every realm of the Universe, coming together, embracing each one of you, embracing the Earth, embracing the Light Beings of your Oceans.

You have been told of the new *"Song of the Earth"* that will ring out at the time of the Equinox, that will permeate every atom of your Earth and of your Being, and you will be uplifted by this *symphony of Love, this symphony of Oneness*.

We are in such joy at this time, we have all been a part of your Planet at one time or another, we all know what each of you is going through as you seek the true Light of Love within yourself, and we reach out to uplift you, to join with you, to lift the Earth into a Dimensional Frequency of Light that will enable all of us to be together once more in the Oneness of all that is.

Dear Hears, we invite you now, at this moment, to lift yourselves into the embrace of Shambhala and to spend some time with us in the lead up to the Equinox, to rest in the embrace of your friends, your brothers, your sisters, your Guides, your Masters, ALL are One at this time.

So come, come join us now, and BE a part of something magical and magnificent as the whole of the Earth expands into Light and lifts into its new place amongst the Stars.

Feel the Love we share with you at this time, and will continue to share with you until the Equinox, when once again we will unify in the *Oneness of all that is*.

(15th September 2014)

8

CONSCIOUSNESS LEADS TO AWARENESS, AWARENESS LEADS TO ENLIGHTENMENT AND ENLIGHTENMENT LEADS TO PEACE

(The gathering opens with the Sounds of the Tibetan Bowls, the Blessings Chimes and the Drum)

Greetings, Dear Hearts, we are the Masters of Shambhala

It is such a delight to be with you once more in the lead up to your Equinox.

As you have already been told by Tarak and Margot there is a new energy flowing into the Earth Planet at this time which will come to full force upon your Equinox, an Arcturian Peace Energy drawn from many different Planetary Systems within the Universe and gifted to Earth Mother through the

Songlines of the Earth, the 12 major Songlines of the Earth.

We are aware, Dear Hearts, that you have given names to each of these Songlines based on the Sculptures at Sundown Hill, it is a good and easy way to remember the Songlines, it gives them ... personality, shall we say. All 12 Songlines are equal and you have been give some general information as to the path they take as they move around the Earth Planet to embrace Earth Mother, to become a part of Earth Mother, but at this time we wish to draw your attention to one particular Songline. This Songline is the one that you have called *"Rainbow Serpent".*

You may recall, Dear Hearts, that the route that this particular Songline takes around the Planet moves from Sundown Hill to Willow Springs, the 'Energy Gateway' that you have worked with for many years, then on to the Crystal Mountain – Mount Gee – which again you have worked with for many years, and worked with the *Unicorn Temple* in another Dimensional Frequency beneath that Crystal Mountain. It then moves through King's Canyon, another place sacred to the Aboriginal people of your land. Then it moves to Tibet, and in particular to *Mount Kailash*. Then through Russia to the

North Pole and down the spine of North America to Machu Picchu.

As you have been told many times, Dear Hearts, each of the Songlines contains many Sacred Places, many 'Gateways', many Energy Vortices, some you know and some you do not, some you work with and some you do not. As we have just said, you work on this particular Songline – the *Rainbow Serpent Songline* – with the Gateways at Willow Springs and at Mount Gee, but you have little or no knowledge of the special Energy Gateway at *Mount Kailash* in Tibet, and it is that particular Energy Gateway that we wish to talk to you about today.

At the beginning of time when life began to form upon the infant Earth Planet, the Energy Gateway at *Mount Kailash* was the gateway through which the energy of *'Consciousness'* came to the Planet from the *Divine Source*, for without Consciousness life has no meaning, Consciousness is necessary for growth, for development, for progress, all of which the infant Earth was undertaking. You see, Dear Hearts, *Consciousness leads to Awareness, Awareness leads to Enlightenment and Enlightenment leads to Peace.*

Many of your early civilizations were keenly aware of the existence of this Energy Gateway – ***Mount Kailash*** – although it may not have been called that by all those who were aware of it, it has many names for the same doorway of Consciousness. But over time the knowledge of this place became lost to civilizations that followed, but not completely lost, the concept of Consciousness and Enlightenment remained as part, if you like, of the DNA of the life forms that were created upon the Earth Planet, particularly the life form of Humanity. So even today, though there is little knowledge of this place, there are still four of what you call 'religions' who regard this place as extremely Sacred, and each of those 'religions' have as their centerpiece the word ***'Enlightenment'***. The belief system is one of seeking Enlightenment, the premier amongst these of course is what you call Buddhism.

But you may say, "Well, that is the past, why are you drawing this to our attention now?" well, Dear Hearts, the inflow of a new Energy of Peace is of prime importance to the Earth Planet, but Peace Energy without ***'Consciousness'*** simply dissipates, so at the same time as Beloved Tarak and Beloved Margot are facilitating the inflow of the Arcturian

Peace Energies through the Songlines, *Mount Kailash* is opening to allow the *'Consciousness of Peace'* to flow from the *Creator* into the Songline simultaneously, to ensure that this energy of Peace has as part of its fabric a Consciousness. *Energies impact on matter, Consciousness impacts on Souls.* So the inflow of this new Peace Energy accompanied by the Consciousness of Peace from the Creator, will stir the Planet into a new Enlightened Awakening.

This Consciousness of Peace will flow into the *Rainbow Serpent Songline,* and through that Songline move to Sundown Hill, move to Machu Picchu, and infuse all the other Songlines around the Planet, so that the whole of the Earth Planet is embraced with the Energy of Peace and the Consciousness of Peace.

Imagine if you can, Dear Hearts, the immense power involved in a Peace which has *'Consciousness'*. It doesn't simply *'exist'*, it *'grows'*, it grows towards *'awareness'*.

Humans infused with both the Energy and the Consciousness of Peace will have a growing awareness of how to make Peace a reality, and that will lead to the Enlightenment, and that will lead to a new Frequency of Peace right throughout the Earth, through all life forms, but most importantly, from your point of view, Dear Hearts, throughout Humanity. All life form upon the Earth has Consciousness, Humanity is not alone in this, although it can and does use Consciousness more frequently - though not necessarily more wisely - than other life forms.

So we ask you as you move now towards your Equinox to focus your Hearts, focus your intent on the *Rainbow Serpent Songline,* to empower and embrace the energies of the new *Arcturian Peace*, and also the *Consciousness of Peace* from the *Divine.* Tarak and Margot, of course will be working from this particular Songline for the Temple, the Pyramid of Sound exists upon this Songline - The *Rainbow Serpent.*

Rainbow Serpent, as you may be aware, in your Aboriginal Dreamtime Mythology is part of the creator force for the Earth, so it is not by accident, Dear Hearts, that the Consciousness comes through *Mount Kailash*, which sits upon the *Rainbow Serpent Songline.* So we ask you, Dear Hearts, to join with all those across the Earth and focus your *intent* upon the Songlines. and in particular, upon the ***Rainbow Serpent Songline*** and allow those energies and that Consciousness of Peace to become a part of you.

Dear Hearts, we will be working with you and we will be empowering the Songlines of the Earth with ***OUR*** energies and with ***OUR*** Consciousness.

Blessings be upon each and every one of you.

(17TH March 2017)

9

THE TIME OF DESTROYING THE EARTH MUST COME TO AN END

(The Circle opens with the Sounds of the Tibetan bowl, the Blessings Chimes and the Drum.)

Focus on the new vibrational frequency of the Magenta Light within your Heart, allowing yourself to be lifted up into the Soul Dimension of the Earth Planet, for you have begun a new journey with the Earth Planet, a journey of new frequencies, new vibrations, new Dimensions of Light, all held within your Heart.

Greetings, Dear Hearts, we are the Masters of Shambhala.

We wish to thank you for the work you have done with Beloved Mother Earth in lifting the Earth Planet into its new Cosmic frequency of Light - *no*

longer the Blue Planet, but the Magenta Planet, a Planet of Love and Peace.

We have all been celebrating the leap forward that took place at your Solstice, for yes, Dear Hearts, we were all a part of your ceremonies and your celebrations, and we too in Shambhala have been uplifted by the outflow of Magenta Light. As the Earth itself lifts into its new frequency, Shambhala also is lifted into new frequencies of Light, so we too are beginning a new journey, one of great promise, one of great excitement, so we share with you the Joy of this re-birth of your Planet.

It will of course take some time for the Magenta Light to permeate throughout the Earth and to begin to unwind the old energies and to bring new hope, new expectations, new dreams for the whole of Humanity.

It is important, Dear Hearts, that you spend time focusing your energies on the Light within your Heart, for the journey ahead is a ***Heart*** journey, not a mind journey, and the Heart is filled with Peace, with Love, and with Joy.

Let go of the past - it is so easy to say, but often so difficult to do - but it is important to make the first small steps into this new world of Peace by resonating outwards from yourselves the new Peace energies bubbling and pulsating within your Heart.

No journey is without its hills and valleys, so you will not always feel completely uplifted, but the more you focus upon the energies within your Heart, the easier your climb will be when there are barriers placed in your way by others who are less than Loving, and less than Peaceful. The new Magenta energies will smooth your way, will uplift you, will enable you to see the potential that lies on your new pathway, a pathway of Light, a path full of Joy.

So, Dear Hearts, we implore you – each morning when you awake from your time of rest - to focus immediately on the Magenta Light within your Heart and see it as your own personal doorway into the new Dimensional frequencies. Open it wide, step through that doorway, and know with total certainty that you are in a new Dimension of the Earth – the Soul Dimension of the Earth, and within this Dimension there are no shadows, there are no judgments, there is only Joy and Peace, and the more you practice doing this and holding on to that Magenta Light within your Hearts and resonating forth that Magenta Light, the easier it becomes, and the more permanent it becomes in your life.

Each one of you has come to this Earth Planet at this time to be a part of this re-birthing, because you all came knowing that your Soul Dimension could lift the Earth Planet into It's Soul Dimension, through the resonance of Love and Joy.

So move forward on your journey, Heart based, always Heart based, and embrace all those around you with the Divine Love within your Heart, and take every opportunity to assist others to see the ***New Soul of the Earth Planet***, that they may find greater Love within their Hearts for the Earth Planet.

The time of destroying the Earth must come to an end, the time to be ***ONE*** with the Earth is ***Now*** and it is ***All*** within your own Heart,

So be Loving, Dear Hearts, in all that you do, in all that you say, in all that you think.

(29th June 2015)

10

BLESSING IS THE ENERGY
OF EQUALITY

(The Circle opens with the Sounds of the Tibetan
bowls and the Blessings Chimes)

*Radiate your Blessings out into the World, lifting
the Hearts of all upon the Earth Planet at this
time.*

**Greetings Dear Hearts, we are The Masters of
Shambhala.**

It is our great delight and our great pleasure to be
with you again this evening to share in the Love
and the Light that you gift to us and to the rest
of Humanity in your daily lives. You may not do
this on a conscious level or in a specific form each
day but you have allowed your Hearts to be open,
radiating forth unconditional Love to ALL, *and this*

is a Blessing, a Blessing for yourselves, as well as a Blessing for others.

It is so important at this time to remain conscious and awakened to all that is happening around you on your Planet, and yet, to not be in judgment of what is happening, but to simply radiate forth your Blessings of Love, your Blessings of Peace, your Blessings of Joy, for it is as these energies come together that the Earth begins its transition into Higher Frequencies of Light, drawing with it those who have yet to awaken.

It is not for each of you to make judgments about those who are not as yet awakened, know, Dear Hearts, that when the time is right for them they will indeed awaken, for the Light and the Love and the Peace and the Joy is moving within each one of them, providing guidance on their journey, and their journey of awakening is as important as yours - but YOU must focus upon your own journey.

That is not a selfish thing, it is an important and desirable happening, for when you focus upon your own journey you do not look at others with judgment, you simply acknowledge that all upon the Earth are moving in their own way and in their own time and on their own journey, and they are contributing to the Ascension of the Earth in their own way, sometimes as Conscious Beings of awakened Light, sometimes subconsciously as they strive within themselves to awaken from the deep sleep of separation and dis-unity. They will be moved by the energies of ONENESS that are beginning to permeate the whole of the Earth Planet and they will respond to the promptings of their own Souls.

So follow your own path, Dear Hearts, follow your own dreams and allow others to follow theirs.

You will not all be at the same level of attainment, but that is not important. What is important is that *each is equal on the journey, wherever they are on that journey they are equal, of equal importance, of equal relevance.*

Equality is not sameness - Equality is acceptance.

Can you imagine, Dear Hearts, if everyone arrived at the gateway at the same time? It would be chaos, would it not? Some may arrive early, some may arrive late and that is okay, in fact it helps in the Ascension process for people to be awakening at different times and at different levels to ensure that the route is smooth, uncomplicated, you are not stuck in a traffic jam!

You are welcome at any time, Dear Hearts, to visit with us at Shambhala - some rest and recuperation for the next stage of your journey - for we know and we understand, Dear Hearts, that there are times when you feel that you are not moving at all, that you are in some kind of hiatus. At those times, Dear Hearts, visit with us in Shambhala, re-energize your commitment by sitting with the Masters and sharing your wisdom with them as they will share their wisdom with you, for each has a unique contribution to make for their own journey and for the journey of others, *but not in a directive way, not in a controlling way, but simply in a sharing way.*

Acknowledge daily, Dear Hearts, the Blessings that you possess, the Blessings you choose to share with others, the Blessings that others choose to share with you, for *in the act of Blessing you share the deepest Love possible, the unconditional non-judgmental Love, for Blessing is the energy of equality*.

We thank you for accepting us into your Hearts tonight and we look forward to sharing again within this Circle, within Shambhala, for *WE ARE ALL ONE* on the journey of Ascension.

(30th June 2014)

11

EVERY THING YOU LOOK UPON IS A GIFT OF BLESSING IN YOUR LIFE

(The Circle opens with the Sounds of the Tibetan bowls and the Blessings Chimes.)

Embrace the blessedness within yourself, and express that blessedness through the vibration of blessing others with whom you share this beautiful Planet, for it is so important to acknowledge blessings in every aspect of your life, indeed, to see and acknowledge that *every part of your life is a blessing.*

It is only when you accept and acknowledge that everything within your life is a blessing that you begin to lose your need for judgment.

Events that happen in your lives may be perceived as challenges, but those challenges still represent a blessing for your growth. Nothing that is presented to you in your Earthly life existence is for anything other than your own growth, your own learning, your own awakening, so, Dear Hearts, it is time to let go of the duality of judgment - that things that happen within your life are either 'good' or 'bad' - *everything in your life is experience, and from experience comes growth.*

When you perceive everything in that Light you will have the realization that everything is a blessing, and that indeed you are merely a reflection of the blessings that exist upon your Planet, so as you embrace the blessings around you, you begin to share those blessings with others who may not have the sight and the understanding that you have.

Greetings, Dear Hearts, we are the Masters of Shambhala.

It is so good to be with you in a new year, a year of such promise, a year of such expectation. Perception will change within each and every one of you. As we have just explained to you, all of life upon the Earth is a blessing in one form or another, it is only your perceptions that need to change, to let go of the judgments of duality and to embrace All that is - the

ONENESS that you and the Earth Planet have now become.

The Blessings Chimes were gifted to you so that you may Sound them out into the world to awaken all of Humanity to the existence of blessings in their lives. In the past, Dear Hearts, you have perceived blessings as an occasional happening that enlightens the darkness of your day to day lives, when in reality it is the permanent energy of your life. You are constantly blessed by the sun, by the moon, by the rhythms of the Earth, by the oceans, *everything you look upon is a gift of blessing in your life.*

If you absorb that thought for just a moment and feel how your body reacts to the realization that it is blessed, that it is filled with blessings, then your whole life existence operates on the level of blessedness.

You have been told for too long that 'pain and suffering is your daily lot, that you have fallen from grace'. This has never been the case, you have always existed in the embrace of the Creator and the Creator is pure Love, and if you are in the embrace of pure Love permanently, *That* indeed is blessedness, so allow yourself to let go of what you have been told in the past and to embrace anew in this new year the blessedness of your existence, of your life.

Look around you, Dear Hearts, look around you at all the amazing aspects of your world, and we say to you *"how can you look upon the beauty of your world and not feel blessed?"*

Look upon the oceans, see how they change, see how they glisten, see how they move, see how they vibrate. Look at all the plants and the animals, each perfect for what it is on the Earth to do, *That* is blessedness. It is the 'perception' that changes, what you have been taught through many lifetimes upon your Planet by those who have sought to control you. Their time of power is gone, Dear Hearts.

This is the time of acknowledging and accepting your blessedness and the blessings of your life - a life, Dear Hearts, that you have chosen, and chosen wisely through your Soul Being.

When you awake each morning go within and embrace the blessedness inside you and then open your eyes and look out upon your world and see that blessedness reflected back to you by all you see.

This a total change of attitude - perception and perspective - and when all of you embrace the blessedness within, you will change the future of the Earth Planet, for you create the reality of your life through your actions, and your actions are governed by how you perceive yourselves, and if, Dear Hearts, you can perceive yourself as blessed, the world becomes a totally different place, for you embrace all that is good, all that is positive, all that is beautiful and you live without judgement. You paint the Earth in the Magenta Light of Love, and you begin to smile, and everyone else notices your smile and begins to smile back to you, for you see, Dear, Hearts, Love and Joy are contagious, so we ask you tonight

Are you ready to begin this new part of your journey with a smile on your face and with blessedness in your Heart?

(11th January 2016)

12

EACH OF US HOLDS A DIFFERENT SPACE, A DIFFERENT PORTION OF THE WHOLE

(The Circle opens with the Sound of the Tibetan Bowls and the Blessings Chimes)

Greetings Beloveds, We are the Masters of Shambhala.

Allow yourself to feel uplifted in Spirit, that you may join our Circle as we gather at Shambhala for the meeting of the Masters. For tonight, instead of us visiting you, we are inviting each and every one of you to visit with us, for *we are the Masters of Shambhala,* and we gather at this place, at this time each year to celebrate and embrace the energies of Enlightenment.

When you walked your Labyrinth and opened the Portal of Enlightenment, you opened the pathway to Shambhala, for in times past you have regarded Shambhala as a place that is not a part of you, a place where Masters meet and greet and make decisions, but now, Dear Ones, it is a part of you.

You have uplifted in your energies and now walk with the Masters and talk with the Masters, and share the Love within your Heart with the Masters, and you will quickly come to know Dear Ones that *you yourselves, are Masters*. You have always been Masters - you simply did not recognize yourself as such. No one can make you what you are not.

Moving through the Portal of Enlightenment allowed you to see your own Divine nature, allowed you to embrace your own Divine talents and wisdom, and allowed you to accept yourself as a Master of Divine Energies.

We have always been equal, Dear Ones, but we are filled with joy that you have finally accepted that equality within yourself, and come now to be with us, to work with us for the upliftment of the Earth itself and all upon her.

Each one of you has much to contribute to the Enlightenment of the Earth, to the advancement of the Earth, and it is all contained within the Love in your Hearts.

So tonight, Dear Ones, we welcome you to Shambhala, and invite you to sit with us awhile, to share the trials and tribulations of your journeys upon the Planet Earth, for within your journeys is much learning for you, and much learning for us, for each of us holds a different space, a different portion of the whole.

Without your contribution we cannot complete the Transcendence of this beautiful Planet, and that is our task, Dear Ones, and always has been our task, to assist the Earth to ascend into its mighty state of Divinity within the Cosmos.

Feel the Love within Shambhala embracing you, feel it touching you, caressing you, and know you are home – *for home is the Love within your Heart*. As you awaken to your own Divinity and embrace that Love within your Heart, you become the Oneness of all that is.

Simply allow yourselves to be the Love within your Heart, and feel the Love and the Light of all the others around you – not one in competition with another, but all joined as one, for *in Love there is no competition, there is only acceptance and gratitude, and joyfulness and harmony.*

Feel it now in every fibre of your Being as you walk the halls of Shambhala, greeting those you have connected to many times before in your conscious and your subconscious worlds.

FEEL THE LOVE

Feel the vibration of the new frequencies of Light resonating through you, and listen to the Sound of your Heart as it sings your new melodies of Light.

(Those within the circle Sounded in Unity)

Embrace fully the energies of Shambhala, and walk the Earth in your own full Mastership, for YOU ARE ALL DIVINE, AND WE ARE ALL ONE.

Blessings be upon you.

(23rd April 2012)

13

"LOVE" TRULY RULES THIS PLANET OF YOURS

(The Circle opens with the Sounds of the Tibetan Bowls and the Blessings Chimes)

Greetings, Dear Hearts, we are the Masters of Shambhala.

Embrace the Sound vibrations of Joy, for it is the energy of Joy that pervades this Circle this evening - the Joy that comes from lifting "Love" from the emotion of your spleen to the energy of your Heart, as Beloved Sananda suggested at your gathering last week. It is time to redefine the word "Love" in your minds.

It is time to let go of "Love" as an emotional response to events on your Planet, and to lift it once more into the essence of energy - energy which has the power to change everything.

In the depths of your duality when "Love" was merely a response - its power was limited. ***Once you embrace "Love" as an energy - its power is overwhelming,***

It becomes a fire in your Soul,
    It becomes a fire within your whole Being, and
        It uplifts you into Joyfulness.

Tonight as you sit on the eve of the day much of Humanity embraces as a celebration of "Love", it is important to activate this redefinition of the word "Love".

We are all aware of how Humanity, over eons of time, have changed the perceptions of these special days into commercial prospects. *Sananda* mentioned "Love" as a currency in relationships, and this day of Valentine when "Love" is celebrated, has become a currency, and as you look upon it, you will see overwhelmingly, Humans seeking, judging themselves on the basis of what they receive as a symbol of this thing called "Love".

It is time to redefine the word "Love".

What better day to start than the day of 'Valentine', and begin from the moment you awaken on that day to express the energy of "Love", in place of the emotion of "Love".

As you awaken from your dream time, take a moment to place the whole of the Earth within your Heart, and bless it with the "Divine Love" within your Heart, and take a moment to place all the creatures and the Beings upon your Earth, within your Heart, and bless them, one and all – those you know - those you do not know - those you like - those you do not like.

Embrace them all with the energy of "Love", but do not forget first and foremost, to place yourself within your Heart, and bless your own Being, gift yourself what you are willing to gift to others. As you do this you will find you no longer require the validation of others to know the "Love" within your Heart.

We do not seek to change completely your celebrations of this special day. It is important to show your "Love" to others, to embrace those who are close to you, those within your immediate families, those who you have special feelings for, but you do that unconditionally, and you do not judge yourself on the basis of what is returned to you.

Think of yourself now, awakening on your day of Valentine, embracing the Earth, embracing all upon the Earth, surrounding them with the "Divine Unconditional Love" within your Heart.

As you embrace them with this energy, feel the upliftment, feel the fulfillment, feel the Joy and the Bliss, that simply embracing all with your "Love" creates.

This is but the start - the beginning of redefining the word "Love" in your minds, and therefore in your lives.

> You may wish to begin each day from then on with the same ritual of bringing the Earth into your Heart, and blessing it with "Love", bringing all of Humanity into your Heart and blessing them with "Love", bringing all the creatures of the Earth into your Heart, and blessing them with "Love".

This will enable you to create an expansion of the "Love" energy within yourself. The more you share, the more you feel, the more you grow - and you become an integral part of all that is.

As you do this, all life becomes Sacred, all shadows and tentacles of fear and anger are dissolved.

"Love" truly rules this Planet of yours.

We are the Masters of Shambhala and we come to you now with this message of "Love" and we bless you.

(13th February 2012)

14

IT IS TIME TO OPEN YOUR HEARTS TO ALL BEINGS OF LIGHT UPON THE EARTH

(The circle opens with the Sounds of the Tibetan Bowls)

Allow the vibrations of the bowls to fill every aspect of your Being, uplifting you into your Soul Dimension, and look out across the Earth from the vantage point of your Soul Dimension and see the incredible Light that is flooding the Earth at this time, the *Light of Divine Love*, and as you look around your Earth Planet see the Hearts of Humanity opening to receive this *Light of Divine Love*, and as you watch, more and more pinpoints of Light appear in different parts of your Earth, as greater and greater numbers of Humanity open to the Divine Love energies within themselves, and openly embrace the *Light of Divine Love* being shared with the Earth at this time by the Cosmos.

Feel the pulsations of those Lights ever increasing across your Planet, and feel the change of energy within and upon the Earth as the *Light of Divine Love* becomes the *Dominant* energy of the Earth, erasing fear and hatred, and embracing acceptance and respect - one for another.

Greetings Dear Hearts, we are the Masters of Shambhala.

You are beginning your usual journey towards your Equinox, you begin that journey with the day that you call your Valentine's Day, when the Light of Love becomes paramount throughout your Earth, and it is the beginning time for the lead up towards your Equinox, a time when great changes will take place upon your Planet, when you will begin to accept and embrace your brothers and sisters from the Ocean Dimension, those you have worked with for so long.

You may recall, Dear Hearts, that at the last Equinox you brought in a new Sound Vibration for the *Light Beings of the Ocean Dimension*, and that has spread from Being to Being within the Ocean Dimension, and at this coming Equinox the Light Beings of the Ocean Dimension will begin to speak to your Hearts in a language of Love, and you will feel yourselves awakening aspects of your Being you have never recognized before, a feeling of such Oneness, of such Unity that you will wonder why it has taken so long for you to recognize that you are ALL *One* upon this Planet. *You may be different in appearance, you may be different in the way you conduct your lives, but you are all a part of the Oneness of Love.*

It will be time for you to let go of your feelings or your beliefs of the superiority of Humanity over all other life forms on the Earth Planet, and to begin to embrace them and accept them, and in so doing begin to share the wisdom that they possess from their many lifetimes upon your Earth.

There are times, Dear Ones, when you look to the stars and wonder about the assistance that is there, but you do not look at other Dimensions upon and within your Earth and ask the same questions ! and until you do this, Dear Hearts, until you embrace the Oneness of All that is on this Planet, you cannot expect to reach out into the Universe, for you are still living in a Dimension of separation, a Dimension of 'superiority'. *You presume as Humans that you are different because you have minds and intelligence. Dear Hearts, you have no idea of the wisdom and the intelligence that other Beings of Light on your Planet possess !*

It is time to open your Hearts, to open your understanding and acceptance of all other Beings of Light upon the Earth, and when you do this and you become One complete Unity, THEN Dear Hearts, then you will look to the stars and you will be greeted by the stars as a Planet of Love, as a Planet of acceptance and understanding.

The Beings of Light within your Oceans are not play things for your pleasure, Dear Hearts, they are Beings of great wisdom and they often seek through their SOUND to communicate that wisdom to you - but in your belief system of 'superiority', you do not listen !

The energies permeating the Earth Planet between now and the Equinox are designed to open you, to open your Hearts and your minds to the Oneness of all that is upon the Earth, and within the Earth.

It is time, Dear Hearts, for you to set aside your concepts of 'superiority'. and to open your Hearts to the greater wisdom of the Earth itself, and of the many, many Beings of Light upon the Earth and within the Earth.

The new Dimension of Oneness REQUIRES YOU to open your Hearts with humility, and embrace the wisdom of others.

When we speak of the Equinox, Dear Hearts, we are not saying that in one moment upon that day you will suddenly awaken to all that is. The Equinox will provide you with an opportunity to do so. The choice, the free will remains with you, and you have to ask yourselves *"Do I wish to continue to feel 'superior' ? and continue to be separate ? or do I choose to open with 'Loving Intent' to the wisdom of ALL?"*

And if you choose to open, Dear Hearts, all you need to do is listen, Listen to your Heart, for it is through your Heart that the communication will occur with all other ***Beings of Light*** upon the Earth. Begin with your Valentine's Day and let the Love build within your Hearts, and let the doors that you have held closed within your Hearts to other Beings, be opened. ***Do not be afraid to admit to yourselves, Dear Hearts, that all are equal, all are One.***

<u>*Embrace Love.*</u>
<u>*Embrace all.*</u>

(10th February 2014)

15

RAINBOW CHORUS OF
LIGHT AND SOUND

(The Circle opens with the Sounds of the Tibetan
Bowls and the Blessings Chimes)

Feel yourselves bathed in the flickering coloured
Lights upon the table before you, drawing into
yourself the colour that you most need at this
time to enlighten your Heart. The spectrum of
colour on your Planet that you view through
your Human eyes is but a small part of the full
spectrum of colour in the Cosmos, so give your
Heart permission to reach out for the appropriate
colour vibration that it needs and requires at this
time, whether it be a colour you perceive with your
Human eyes or a colour you can but imagine. The
importance of colour cannot be over emphasized,
it melds with the Sounds within your body and it
uplifts your Spirit.

The rainbow that you perceive in your sky is just a minute part of the vast colours of the Universe and yet each time you see such rainbows it lifts your Spirit, it lifts your Heart, it creates Joy within YOU, within your physical Dimension, but through your Heart you can embrace the other colour rainbows of the Cosmos through your multi-dimensional self, it simply requires you to open your Heart and allow yourselves to BE the multi-dimensional Being that you are in reality - although you rarely perceive in your human form.

Greetings, Dear Hearts, we are the Masters of Shambhala.

We come tonight to embrace each and every one of you with the Cosmic Rainbow of colour, that your 'Energy Beings' may be filled with the brightest most vivid colours that exist in the whole of your Universe, the whole of your Cosmos. They may not be seen by the Human eyes upon your Planet, but they still exist within you if your Heart has called them into your Being, and each one of those colours vibrates as a part of you and radiates forth to become a new Light for someone else.

Each individual is activated by a different colour frequency, so YOU, through your multi coloured Light, will assist in the activation of the Light within other Beings on a scale much greater and vaster than your minds can possibly imagine.

Just as 'Sound' is not contained solely within the structures of your musical terms upon the Earth, the range of sound is vast. There are creatures, animals upon your Planet who hear sounds that Humans do not, and yet cannot hear sounds that Humans can. This is part of the wonders of your Planet, Dear Hearts, every Being, every animal, every creature is different, resonates with a different Light, resonates with a different Sound, and yet you are all a part of the ONE.

Colour and Light are of great significance in the Ascension of the Earth Planet at this time. As you have already been told, the new *'Song of the Earth'* is vibrating its colour through your Earth, melding together the Songlines of the Earth and the Crystalline Grids of the Earth so that every part of your Planet is awakened to the whole spectrum of the Cosmos.

Do not worry, Dear Hearts, if you perceive that you are limited in your appreciation of Sound or Colour, what is important is to know within your Heart that everything that exists in the Cosmos exists also within your Heart, every colour frequency, every Sound vibration exists within your Heart, but you, in your Human form and in your current lifetime, are responsible for what you allow to radiate forth from YOU.

We come tonight to ask you to open your Hearts totally and vibrate every single colour of the Cosmos and every single Sound of the Cosmos out into the world. The person standing next to you may receive one colour, the person in another part of the world may receive another colour or another Sound, but each one of them comes from within your Heart.

It is not by accident, Dear Hearts, that colour has been made such a focus within Pendragon, for it is part of the role that each of you - as a Circle of power - has to operate throughout the Earth, By gathering many Hearts together you radiate more and different colours and more and different Sounds, and different life forms upon your Planet receive them and feel uplifted by them. *The power of the ONE is also the power of the WHOLE.*

Many times you look out upon your world and you do not see the bright colours of upliftment, you see only the shadows of 'no colour', and then Hearts open and come together and they create a new power, a new Light, a new Sound of freedom to BE, a Joyfulness.

You have seen it today, Dear Hearts, as many people in the place you call Paris have come together, opened their Hearts and sung and Sounded and spoken and radiated forth the power of Love, the power of compassion, the power of *UNITY* and they have created a wave of colour that has moved across the face of the Earth, touching Humans in every country. So from that one moment of 'no-colour', of 'darkness', has sprung forth a new radiant Rainbow of Love.

So when you look out upon your world, Dear Hearts, look beyond the 'no-colour' and connect to the Hearts of Sound and Colour and *build Bridges of Light between countries, between individuals, between Planetary systems,* for you are not alone in the Cosmos, there are many Beings on many Planets and many Stars, who look to the Earth and see what is happening, and they too are uplifted with Joy as they see Hearts opening and coming together and becoming a ***Rainbow Chorus of Light and Sound.***

Allow your Hearts to be fully open at all times. We know this is difficult upon your Planet, for you do not want to accept the possibilities of pain and suffering when you open your Hearts and become defenseless, but in reality, Dear Hearts, you are never defenseless, for the Love within your Hearts is your protection, it is your filter, and if you walk forth upon your Planet with a totally open Heart, there is nothing and I say again, NOTHING that can hurt you, for Love is an indestructible energy.

Let it sing in your Hearts and let your Rainbows of Colour reach out to everyone and everything upon the Earth.

(12th January 2015)

16

FEEL, EMBRACE, BECOME THE HEALING LIGHT OF DIVINE LOVE

(The Circle opens with the Sounds of the Tibetan Bowls and the Blessings Chimes.)

We call into this Circle tonight the Healing Light of Divine Love, and connect each of our Hearts to this Healing Light of Divine Love, and focus that Light on all those in need of Healing at this time, those of our friends and our families, those beyond our immediate Circle, connecting our Hearts, strengthening the Healing Light of Divine Love and radiating forth across the Earth, reaching out to all other Beings of Light on and within the Earth, on and within the Oceans of the Earth, creating wave after wave of Divine Love reaching into the Hearts of *ALL* upon the Earth, allowing the Light of Divine Love to find a resonance within each Heart.

FEEL, EMBRACE, BECOME the Healing Light of Divine Love.

Greetings, Dear Hearts, we are The Masters of Shambhala,

We greet you tonight with the deepest Love and we ask you to focus on the Oneness that you are, allowing that Light of Divine Love that you have called into your Circle to cement the Oneness of all of you, and of all those connected to you in that Oneness, for it is the power of the whole that creates the Light and the Love and uplifts all upon your Planet into the realms of your Souls.

Your journey of Ascension is your journey of your Soul Dimension, Dear Hearts, allowing your perceptions to rise, to allow the Light within your Hearts to rise and be directed from within your Soul Dimension.

This is a time of growing Unity on your Planet, a coming together into Oneness. It is part of the reason why, Dear Hearts, you are noticing more frequently any aspects of life on your Planet which is not in Oneness, the disharmony and disunity that appears to be prevalent in some of your countries, is simply you becoming more aware of Oneness, and of the power of togetherness, the power of caring and loving.

Often, Dear Hearts, you are shown aspects of life simply to allow you to know the difference, to allow you to share the power within YOUR Hearts with others that need to find the Light and the caring that being in Oneness brings to your World.

It is why, Dear Hearts, we have spoken to you many times before about letting go of judgments. *Life is about observing and embracing with Love.* It is not about judgments, for judgments are intensely personal. You are looking at scales of perception, you are looking at one course of action over another course of action, and yet both courses of action may lead you to the same place, each has its own merits, each has its own perceived failings, but each is Light in its own way.

So let go of judgments, Dear Hearts, look out upon your World, acknowledge what is happening, embrace with Love and seek the healing of the Earth in the healing of yourself.

You are moving into the time of the Wesak, the time of the Buddha, the Enlightened One. It is your time, for you, each and every one of you are the Enlightened Ones - and being Enlightened does not mean being better than. *Being Enlightened means accepting the Divinity of all that is, and giving and sharing your Love freely without judgment.*

Here at Shambhala we celebrate this great occasion of Enlightenment and we invite you to do the same.

Dear Hearts, we all have a role to play, we all have gifts to share. Share your gifts of Love and Light now and focus the intent of your Hearts on the Healing Light of Divine Love, and allow that to radiate forth across the Earth touching ALL, offering ALL the opportunity to be ONE.

(12th May 2014)

17

DIVINE LOVE IS THE MOST POWERFUL HEALING ENERGY IN THE UNIVERSE

(The Circle opens with the Sounds of the Tibetan Bowls and the Blessings Chimes.)

We focus the Light within our Hearts on those we have placed within the Circle tonight for Healing, for Love, for Enlightenment and we also place the Earth Planet within the Circle, that the Light from our Hearts may irradiate the Earth Planet with the energies of Divine Love, for *Divine Love is the most powerful healing energy in the Universe,* and so with the Light from within our Hearts we embrace the Earth Planet and all upon the Earth Planet with the energies of Divine Love for the healing of the *Souls* of all upon the Earth, and with the Light from within our Hearts we seek to open the Hearts of all others upon the Earth that they too may contribute the Divine Love energies to the healing of the Earth.

Greetings Dear Hearts, we are the Masters of Shambhala.

Once more we have come together at Shambhala to gaze upon the Earth Planet, to embrace with our Love the Light Beings upon and within the Earth who are working, and simply ***BEING*** at this time in their Light and in their Divine Love, for the upliftment and Ascension of the Earth and all upon the Earth.

Every unique Being upon the Earth Planet is part of the whole, is contributing to the whole, but it is the whole itself that works the magic upon the Earth.

Throughout the Earth Planet there are many, many Circles much like this one who come together from time to time, some with great regularity, to fuse their Hearts into a more powerful energy to assist in the Enlightenment and the Ascension of the Earth, to assist in the Awakening of others upon the Earth Planet, and we commend and embrace each and every one of these Circles of Light.

Much can be achieved when two Hearts are brought together. When there is more than two Hearts the power of that Light increases dramatically and when within that Circle there is a focus of Light, a focus of intent, great magic can be achieved upon the Earth.

You may feel at times that your gathering together has no impact on what is happening upon your Planet, for the work you do is very rarely reported, but that does not mean that it does not exist, and that it is not powerful, and that it is not purposeful.

Just as we come together in Council at Shambhala, you come together in Council in your Circles, the unique Light of each individual joining with the others to create a powerful energy of Love.

We watch, we listen, we see what you do not see with your Human eyes - but you know with your Human Hearts - the Light that you are spreading across the plains and mountains of the Earth and through the Oceans of the Earth is amazing to behold, and from time to time we come to speak with you, to ask you to assist in certain projects that may be deemed to be important at a particular time and you have never let us down, Dear Hearts, and *we express our thanks and our gratitude to you for all the work that you do for the Earth, for Humanity, for the Universe.*

You are all multidimensional Beings of Light and as you become more and more aware and more and more accepting of your Divine birthright, the more powerful are the energies you radiate.

So although placing in your Circle the names of those you Love is a symbolic gesture, it is much more than that, Dear Hearts, you will impact with your energies upon those you have named, those you have thought of, and of course, Planet Earth itself.

Sometimes, Dear Hearts, you do things because you have learned to do them, you do not actually necessarily believe that you are having the effect that you desire, we are here to tell you tonight that you do indeed have the effect that you desire.

Now, Dear Ones, you cannot change the life span of others, but that is not important, for *there is no life and death, there is only a transition between one part of your life and another part of your life,* so in giving Love to those who you perceive as leaving your Earthly life, you are gifting them immeasurable energies of Love for the next stage of their journeys, the journeys that they will choose.

So, Dear Hearts, continue to embrace all with the healing energies of Divine Love and then allow them to choose how best to utilize those energies, but *never doubt for one moment, Dear Hearts, the effectiveness, the power of the Love you gift so freely.*

Healing is an interesting word, it has certain connotations in your languages, but the energy of healing goes far beyond the physical. *The energy of healing is the empowerment of the individual to choose their journey, to choose their life, to choose their Dimension of existence.* All too often you limit healing to a perception of physicality.

We ask you to open up the perception of healing to the embracing of all, to the embracing of your multidimensionality, to an acceptance of your Soul journey as well as your physical journey.

Focus your Hearts once again, Dear Ones, focus your minds on what you have placed within the Circle and now *allow* others to make their choices. Gift them your Love, gift them your Joy, gift them your Acceptance and allow them to Be who they are meant to Be. Allow the Earth Planet to Be what the Earth Planet is meant to Be, not just your own perspective of what it is meant to Be.

Gift your LOVE without condition, without expectation, for LOVE is the ultimate energy of freedom.

(18th August 2014)

18

YOU ARE PART OF THE FLOW OF WISDOM AND KNOWLEDGE, AND YOU CONTRIBUTE AS MUCH AS YOU RECEIVE

(The Circle opens with the Sounds of the Tibetan bowls and the Blessings Chimes)

The Sound of Love fills this Circle tonight and expands outwards in waves of Light and Love to bless the whole of Humanity and to bless Beloved Earth Mother, for you and the Earth are in Oneness of purpose at this time, the purpose of Ascending into higher and higher Dimensional Frequencies, releasing all the darkness of the past and embracing Divine Light and Divine Love, and feeling that within your Hearts as Divine Peace and Divine Joy, *for in Oneness there is growth, in Oneness there is expansion, in Oneness there is Ascension.*

There is much that is happening in the world at this time that may cause each and every one of you to feel trapped in the old energies, but, Dear Hearts, this is because you have Ascended beyond those energies and can now see them for what they are, whereas before, Dear Hearts, you were so much a part of those old energies that you failed to recognize them when they were in front of your eyes. Now, as you sit high in your Soul Dimension, you see what is old and no longer necessary struggling to hold on as the world and the Earth Planet passes them by, and yes Dear Hearts, they are seeking to make as much noise as possible to attract your attention, to draw you back into the fold of darkness, but this cannot be, for each and every one of you have moved on into the wondrous beauty of your own Light and your own Love, and we here in Shambhala applaud the purposefulness you are showing on your journeys.

Greetings, Dear Hearts, we are the Masters of Shambhala.

Last week, Dear Hearts, you were shown through this one (*David*) that Shambhala exists not only in Higher Dimensional Frequencies, but also deep within the Heart of Earth Mother, for just as you have been told to look within and not to rely on that which is outside of yourself, Earth Mother too needs to look within and be One with the Shambhala of its Heart - *'as above, so below'* - but Dear Hearts, which is above and which is below?

The highest form of energy is within your own Heart, and within the Heart of Earth Mother, so you may perceive that as the high, *'as above',* and you may perceive anything beyond that as the *'so below'.* It is purely a matter of perception, how you perceive the realities of your existence.

It has been hard in the past for your minds to accept the concept that everything is within you, and what is outside of yourself is merely a reflection, a mirror to what exists within your Heart.

Powerful energies are moving to and through and from the Heart of Earth Mother, for growth is not something that comes from the Universe into the Earth, it is also something that comes from the Heart of the Earth and moves out into the Cosmos.

Embrace the Oneness that image portrays. From your Heart, from the Heart of Earth Mother, flows great Wisdom, flows great Light, flows great Love and that will assist and enhance the Ascension of all Beings of Light throughout the Universe, so just as you accept the gifts of energy from the Universe you are constantly giving out to the Universe gifts of your own wisdom.

There is a much greater equality within Oneness than you have ever perceived before, simply because you have believed yourselves to be lesser than, lower than, not as enlightened as other Beings within the Universe, other Planetary Systems within the Universe, but the reality, Dear Hearts, is that you are part of the flow of wisdom and knowledge and you contribute as much as you receive.

We have said to you often times before, *we at Shambhala do not know more than you, we simply know different from you,* and as we share the different wisdom and the knowledge that we all have, we create the momentum for the Ascension of all back to the Heart of the Source, the Divine Creator of all life, but *once more, Dear Hearts, the Divine Creator of all life is not separate from you, you are part of the Divine Creator, and the Divine Creator is a part of you.*

Try to imagine yourselves now as simply part of the flow of Light, the flow of Love, the flow of Joy, the flow of Peace. It is like floating in your Oceans, and feeling yourself to be a part of the Oceans, you begin to understand ONENESS.

Your scientists are now greatly joyful for having perceived some new feature within the Universe that confirms perceptions that they have held for some time. Remember what they are seeing now is a part of you, for everything within the Cosmos is a part of you.

It is not possible for the Human mind to comprehend fully distances which are expressed in terms of 'Light Years', so sometimes you listen to your scientists and you think "how can that be?", you are now seeing something that happened millions of Light Years ago, but think of that in a different way, Dear Heart, in the way that we have expressed to you before - that everything, and I mean everything, is part of the 'now', so 'Light Years' is only a terminology that scientists are using to create an image in your mind. What they are seeing is happening in the 'now' and when you perceive it in that way can you feel the excitement within yourself, that the 'now' is being expanded in your understanding?.

So listen to what your scientists are telling you, and discern their words, their descriptions, as evidence of the existence of the 'now', for time, Dear Hearts, is merely something you have constructed upon the Earth Planet, so everything must be explained relative to this concept of time, but now you are beginning to see the seeds of perceiving these events as being part of the eternal 'now' moment, and when you embrace that, everything falls into place and the Love and the Joy within your Hearts soar into the heavens.

Dear Hearts, we are so delighted to be with you again at this time and to be sharing our understanding of what is happening with the Earth Planet and with Humanity, but *I caution you, Dear Hearts, this is only OUR understanding, YOU must come to your own understandings by delving into the wisdom within your own Hearts,* and then coming to Shambhala and sharing that with us, for as we share our wisdom we increase the size of the picture and we see more and more, and we understand more and more, for We are all a part of the *ONE*.

Blessings, Dear Hearts, and once again we thank you for sharing with us at this time.

(15th February 2016)

19

ALLOW YOUR SOUL HEART
TO SOAR INTO THE LIGHT

(The Circle opens with the Sounds of the Tibetan Bowls and the Blessings Chimes)

Allow yourselves to **BE** in the 'still point' of your Hearts, and simply breathe in the colour vibrations that surround you.

Greetings, Dear Hearts, we are the Masters of Shambhala and we come tonight to invite you to move your Consciousness from your physical vessels to commune with us at Shambhala, allowing your Soul Selves to come to the fore, to assemble with us in Light and Love - *for it is time for each one of you to commit yourselves to the contracts you have signed before you came to the Earth in this lifetime.*

In the lead up to your next Equinox it is a time of re - assessment of your purpose, a time to re - affirm your desires, to re - connect with your Cosmic Being. Do not concern yourselves now with your physical vessels, for they will be protected as you journey with us now to Shambhala, to sit in conference with all your Spirit friends, with all your Spirit family - *your Soul Heart beating once more with the PASSION of your Cosmic Beingness.*

You all know that you came to the Earth at this time with a purpose, with a contract, some of you have completed your contract and need to determine if you intend to create a new contract for your work upon the Earth Planet or if it is time for you to return home.

This is not a momentary decision, it is one that you need to consider carefully between now and the Equinox, for at the time of the Equinox gateways will open to a totally new frequency of Light upon the Earth. You have prepared for this with the Sound vibrations brought into the Earth Planet at the time of the last Equinox. You have prepared for this with the influx of Rainbow Light from the Cosmos, each of these has changed the frequency of the Earth.

Some of you may even now be wondering 'what is your purpose now? where do you go? what do you do?' Many upon your Planet are feeling lost at this time, and that, Dear Hearts, is because many have completed their original contracts, they have brought the Earth Planet to a point in time where specific changes are occurring, they came here to provide the opportunity for those changes, and they are on the threshold of a new adventure, a new journey into higher and higher frequencies of Light.

It is time to ask, Dear Hearts, 'what is within your Heart at this time?'. Do you need the guidance and assistance of your Angelic friends? of your Cosmic family? For now you are being provided with an opportunity to consider your futures, your futures upon or within the Earth, or your futures on your Home Planet.

Can you feel the seeds of Joy rising inside you as you reach this time of critical decision? For unless there is Joy within your Heart, then it is time to leave, but if you are looking at the future of the Earth with feelings of Love and Joy, then your choice is to create a new contract with the Earth - not a contract with us, Dear Hearts, a contract with the Earth.

Allow your Soul Heart to sit within the embrace of Shambhala, rest awhile, look back at what you have achieved in your current contract with the Earth, discuss the potentials, the possibilities of the New Earth journey and your part in that journey, for the changes upon the Earth will be so profound that it will require the most dedicated commitment within your Hearts, if you choose to remain a part of the Earth.

No one but *YOU,* Dear Heart, can make that determination, that decision. No one will judge you badly if you decide it is time for you to return home, time for someone else to take up the responsibilities of assisting the Earth in its further Ascension. *ONLY YOU CAN DECIDE.*

We invite you to be with us at every opportunity, to allow the Higher Frequencies of Shambhala to uplift your vision, to enable you to see the possibilities and the potentials, but also to give you the opportunity to re - connect with HOME.

Feel yourself surrounded and infused by the energies of Pure Love, Pure Peace. There are no shadows within Shambhala, you leave all your Earthly shadows behind with your physical vessel and *you allow your Soul Heart to soar into the Light, to re - acquaint yourself with the essence of who you are.*

Do not feel pressured to make quick decisions, take your time and be sure within your *Soul Heart*, within your *Human Heart.*

BE SURE before you make any commitment to the Earth and to Humanity.

Now let yourselves spend time in the embrace of Shambhala. Embrace your families and your friends and simply

BE IN THE 'STILL POINT' OF YOUR HEART.

(16th February 2015)

20

EACH ONE OF YOU IS A SPARK OF LIGHT

(The Circle opens with the Sounds of the Tibetan Bowls and the Blessings Chimes)

Move your Consciousness deep into the centre of your Being to the place where your Soul resides, and feel the lightness of your Soul Dimension and know that this is the real you, embracing *all* with unconditional Love and with the essence of Joy.

It is important at this time to know that you are *'ONE with all that is'* and that nothing exists outside of yourself that can change what is within your Heart - *you ARE the essence of Love.*

Greetings, Dear Hearts, we are the Masters of Shambhala.

We have been together now for quite some time, since your equinox, for there is so much change taking place within and around and upon the Earth Planet at this time that we need to be almost in constant meditation.

The Earth has awakened to the reality of its own Being and it moves now and breathes now as an Enlightened Being within the Cosmos, and all Beings upon the Earth Planet are feeling the changes that the Earth is going through, and needing to adjust within themselves to the new vibrational frequencies of their surroundings. So your Spiritual friends have come together once more at Shambhala to offer their Love, their Strength, their Joy to each and every one of you, to each and every Being upon and within the Earth Planet, to support you in this time of change.

We are not here, Dear Hearts, to tell you what to do, this has to come from within your own Hearts. Each and every one of you have chosen to be upon the Earth at this time - in part to learn lessons of yourself, but also to offer your Wisdom, your Love, your Comfort to the Earth Planet as it awakens.

Focus if you can, Dear Hearts, on the wholeness of the journey that you are participating in. *Let go of the littleness of your minds,* expand and embrace the whole of the journey. *Move into your Hearts,* ask how can you contribute to the awakening that is occurring upon and within the Earth, and the answer will be, Dear Hearts - *by giving, by sharing, by BEING THE LOVE* that is at the essence of your Heart.

If you focus on Love and radiate that Love, you will be gifting to the Earth Planet more than you realize, you will be strengthening the atmosphere of the Earth and you will be assisting in the awakening of all those Souls who have been upon and within the Earth in times past, that have remained awaiting their awakening.

Each one of you is a spark of Light that the Earth needs to ensure that it reaches its full potential within the Cosmos. There is no judgment from the Earth itself or from your Spiritual friends about the extent of the help that you offer and give, for each spark is important, each spark of Love, each spark of Joy adds to the lustre of the Earth Planet, and as the Earth Planet grows in lustre, you too grow in lustre.

Focus on your Hearts, focus on Love, become a part of the flow of Love and you will become a part of the glow of the Earth Planet as it moves Spiritually and physically through the Ocean of the Cosmos, giving Light, giving Love and giving Hope to so many other Planetary Systems that are watching and waiting for the Love and the Light of the Earth to touch their systems and to begin their awakening.

We invite you to join with us in Shambhala that we may draw our energies together and focus more powerfully upon Earth Mother's Heart and upon the Shambhala within Earth Mother's Heart, and we can then assist the Earth to regain its Light and its Love in full measure.

Embrace your ONENESS and BECOME THE ONENESS OF ALL THAT IS.

(16th May 2016)

21

THIS NEW ENERGY FREQUENCY IS THE ENERGY OF 'UNICORN'

(The gathering opens with the Sounds of the Tibetan Bowl and the Drum)

Greetings, Dear Hearts, we are the Masters of Shambhala.

It has been quite some time, in your Earth time, since we have connected with you in this Sacred Space. Indeed, we have yet to thank you properly for your assistance and your facilitation of the Golden Dolphin energies from Sirius B that were transmitted through the Cetaceans of the Earth Planet into the Crystalline Grid System, the energies of *Joy* more powerful than any the Earth had received before.

No one, not even Earth Mother herself, knew for certain how the Earth and those upon the Earth would react to these powerful energies of **Joy**, and you have no doubt witnessed since your 'Waters of the World' ceremony an increase in a shaking of the Earth's crust in various parts of the Planet, and many of you – 'Sensitives' closely linked to Oceans and Cctaceans   have also felt the power of this energy within your own bodies.

Part of the reason why we have not communicated with you for so long has been that this one (*David*), through whom we speak, has been impacted greatly by these energies, although now he is beginning to recover, and we can at last come through and speak with you. But also there has been another reason, and that is that we, the Masters of Shambhala, and all your archangel friends and your guides have been in conference since this flow of energy to see how we can best assist now that so many changes have taken place upon your Earth Planet.

You see, Dear Hearts, it is not our role to interfere with what is happening upon the Earth, we are here to monitor what is happening and to give assistance if, and when, it is requested by Earth Mother or by Humanity.

This has been a 9 year, in your terminology, a year of endings and preparations for new beginnings, and there have indeed been many changes upon your Planet over this period of time, and there have been many inflows of specific energies to assist in these changes, for it is our role to support the evolution and the Ascension of the Earth Planet and all upon the Earth Planet. So we do not fear change as many Humans fear change, we embrace change and we look for ways of empowering the Light that comes with change.

Now, Dear Hearts, in the very near future there are two more Gateways during which powerful energies will inflow into the Earth and into Humanity. There is, of course, the time, the Gateway that you call the Solstice, this will be the final Gateway of this year of 'endings', and whereas there have been powerful energies during the year to assist you to release the energies of the past that are holding you back, these energies will be less powerful, less disruptive, shall we say. It will be, if you like, a moderation of your current state of balance, so the energies will reflect that, they will not impact you in the way that some of the energies this year have done. So we ask you simply to open your Hearts and embrace the energies and allow the last vestiges of the shadows of darkness, of the energies that no longer support your journey into the Light, to go, releasing them so you are prepared.

Balance is imperative at this time, for there is only a short gap in your Human time scale between the Solstice and the next important Gateway of energy, and this, Dear Hearts, is indeed a most powerful Gateway of energy, it is the Gateway of the 1:1:1

'1' is *"new beginnings",* it is the preparation for the next cycle of 9 years of growth upon the Earth Planet. The energies that will be flowing into the Earth at this time are the energies of *'possibility'*, they are not the energies of releasing that you have been receiving in this year, but the energies of potential and possibility of what you are able to create in the next year, in the '1' year, and the years beyond. It is a time to *'dream'* your dreams and empower your dreams. It is a time to open the doors to the new and exciting possibilities of the future, can you feel the excitement within those energies? even though they are yet, in your time, a few weeks away.

You have prepared yourself, you have released the energies of the past, you have made changes in your life, in your 'attitudes' towards yourself, towards the Earth and towards Humanity as a whole. You have created and established a new starting place, a time of creating new dreams, empowering new visions, for you see, Dear Hearts, the 1:1:1 is moving you into a new vibrational frequency within the Cosmic realms, *this new energy frequency is the energy of the UNICORN*.

Yes, Dear Hearts, you know of Unicorn as some Mystical creature from the past, but Unicorn is an energy in itself, it is a *'Frequency of Light'*. You have been through the Cetacean frequencies, you have been through the Dragon frequencies, and now, on the 1:1:1, you move into the *'UNICORN FREQUENCY'*.

Unicorn – One Horn – ONENESS.

You are being invited into a new frequency of Light that will give greater understanding to the meaning of the word *'Oneness'*. You have received many messages from us and from others within the Cosmic realms over many years that have spoken of *'Oneness'* and tried to differentiate 'Oneness' from 'Sameness', for you are not all suddenly going to be the same Being, you are still going to be all different

Beings, but because you have been releasing many of the darker energies of the past, hatred, disrespect, anger, you have opened yourself to a new awareness of Love, of Joy, and of Oneness, of embracing all upon the Earth, and embracing the Earth itself within that Oneness, accepting, indeed, embracing, enjoying, the 'differences' between Beings of Light upon the Earth Planet, Humans, animals, plant life, the Earth itself, *All are Life Forms, All are Love Forms ! and All contain Joy.*

You may not always feel that your life is filled with *Joy*, particularly as you have been struggling - many of you – with the energies of releasing, and with the energies of change. It is so easy for Humans to become 'down' upon themselves, but from the energies of the 1:1:1 will come a greater understanding of *Joy*, a greater understanding of Love and a greater understanding that 'Oneness is all there is'. Separation may still appear before your eyes, but in your Hearts you will feel a growing sense of Oneness with your neighbors, with your friends, with your relatives, with strangers. Do not let your minds constrict your perceptions of Oneness, move forward with the openness of your Hearts. Your minds will catch up, Dear Hearts, indeed they will, for your attitude to life is not formed within your mind, it is formed within your Heart.

So we come today, to ask you to embrace the energies of the 1:1:1 for these energies, Dear Hearts, are coming to you directly from *'SOURCE'*. This is beyond limiting belief systems, religious systems, this is about the *True Source, - which is Love - which is Joy - which is Oneness.*

Dear Hearts, we look forward to sharing many, many more opportunities within this Sacred Space of communicating and connecting with each and every one of you, and we embrace you with deepest Love and we thank you for persevering through all your Human trials and tribulations, moving into Love and Joy and Peace and Oneness, Keep your hearts open, Dear Ones, and you will feel and see the

BELOVED FREQUENCY OF UNICORN.

(19th December 2016)

22

ONENESS IS NOT ABOUT NON JUDGEMENT, IT IS ABOUT RESPECT, IT IS ABOUT LOVE

(The Gathering opens with the Sounds of the Tibetan bowl, the Drum and the Peace and Harmony Chimes)

Take a moment to relax and clear the clutter from your mind, allowing the Sound Vibrations to move through every atom of your Being, lifting you from the mundane aspects of your world into the higher frequencies of your Soul, for it is within your Soul that you connect and communicate with all other Dimensional frequencies in the Universe and within yourself. Relax - Breathe deeply - Relax - Let your body begin to float, lifting into your Soul Dimension.

Greetings, Dear Hearts, we are the Masters of Shambhala.

It is such a delight for us to be with you again once more, and to share a special Oneness with each and every one of you, for although we recognize and see you as individuals we embrace you as One - One with all Humanity, and One with us.

We do not need to tell you, Dear Hearts, that there is much change taking place upon your Planet, you see it every day, you hear it every day, and you judge it every day, but your judgements are still steeped in the duality of the past, and have yet to become the Oneness of the future, for judgement will always exist within Humanity, the differences are your starting point, what are you judging from? Are you judging from the time of duality ? or are you judging from the time of Oneness ?

Oh yes, Dear Hearts, I know various things have been said to you over the time, and you think that Oneness means no judgements at all, and because of where you have been in your Planet of duality, this makes it difficult for you to comprehend the reality of Oneness.

Oneness is not about non judgement, it is about **Respect,** it is about **Love**. You can still make judgements of yourself, judgements of others, but you do it from deep within your Heart, from deep within the Love within your Heart, you accord every single Being on your Planet, Human and non Human, with Respect, with Honour, and with Love, and when you begin to do that, Dear Hearts, you will find that your judgements become a positive attribute, because they will no longer divide you, they will indeed bind you closer together, for the judgements you make will not be negative judgements. They will be judgements as to 'How best situations can be improved'.

Reality is always about where you start from, Dear Hearts, but you first have to find that. You have to look deep within your Heart and make choices, "am I going to look out upon my World with **Gratitude** and **Love**, or am I going to look out upon my World as a critic of everything I see ?"

Yes, Dear Hearts, many, many changes are taking place, many things which were previously hidden from you are now being revealed, and this is not a comfortable situation, you will be seeing things that you do not necessarily want to see, that do not make you feel Joyful, but you cannot hide from reality, and if you look and see with ***Respect,*** with ***Honour,*** then you can perceive how best the situations can be improved. Judgement is a very strange Beast, Dear Hearts, it begins at home, you start by judging yourselves and it is from within that judgement of yourselves that you begin to judge others, and if you judge yourselves negatively then you will judge others negatively. If you judge yourselves positively, then you will judge others positively.

It would be wonderful, Dear Hearts, to be non judgmental in all things, but we recognize, and you need to recognize, that this is somewhere in the future, when Love has completely taken over the whole of the Earth, and everyone loves everyone because ***Everyone is One !*** but you are in a state of transition on your Planet, you still have to exist within the Dimension in which you reside. It is good, it is important to have ***Visions,*** to have dreams of a better World, and to work towards that better World, but you need to live in the circumstances in which you live, ***so you begin to change your Attitudes first ! Your attitudes towards yourself ! that is Primary !*** for it is the basis of your attitude to everyone else you meet.

You have received many message in the past about healing yourself, and you tend to think of this purely in terms of Physical illnesses, but *healing yourself begins with healing your attitudes to life, your attitudes towards yourself.* We have said many times, Love yourself, and this is, indeed, important, This is the healing that needs to take place, Loving yourselves, finding the Joy within yourselves, and embracing that. Not just looking into yourself and saying "Ah, there's a bit of Joy, there's a bit of love" - *Embrace them, become them,* and when you begin to do that, Dear Hearts, suddenly, almost you might say, miraculously, you see the World through different eyes, and when you see the World through different eyes your judgements begin to change, your judgement becomes *"What can I do, what can we do, to bring Harmony, Peace and Joy to our lives, to our whole Planet ?"*

You are presented within your life many times with situation which demand judgement within you, do not think badly of yourself if you react and greatly give that judgement, but know where that judgement comes from. Is it coming from your own pain? Your own lack of Love for yourself ? and if you realize this is so, that your judgement is a put down on others, rather than an upliftment of others, then Dear Hearts, you know that you have to heal yourself.

The natural state of each and every one of you is *Love*, and your lifetime upon your Planet is about discovering that **Love** and ***BEING that Love,*** because your lifetimes upon your Planet each time are relatively short in your conditioned linear time, you tend to wish to rush thing, and each time you think you have failed in being Loving, you judge yourself negatively, and that makes it more difficult for you to heal yourself, so sit quietly and relax each time a moment like that occurs and go back into your Heart and embrace the Love, the Love of ***yourself***, the Love of life, and bring that again to the surface and look again at the situation and let your judgement now be born of Love - Love of Self.

As in all things, Dear Hearts, it takes practice, it takes standing up and falling down, but I'm sure you remember this as a child, first learning to walk, getting onto your knees, falling over, eventually standing up, falling over. Remember, Dear Hearts, when you fell over as a child you did not lie there and give up, oh no, you knew that if you got up again and conquered your pain and your fear, your fear of failure - oh yes, Dear Hearts, as early as your formative childhood years failure was always a possibility, But you did not allow that to happen ! you stood, and then you walked, and you grew stronger within yourselves.

This is what is happening now, Dear Hearts, *YOU ARE LEARNING TO BE YOUR SOUL !* and that can be frightening, because life creates situations to test how far you have come in becoming your Soul, and each time you fall and you feel that you have failed, you have the choice - do you lie there curled up in a fetal position and give up ? or do you get back on your feet and reach once more for your *SOUL* ?

Eventually, Dear Hearts, you come to the realization that *YOU ARE YOUR SOUL !* you are experiencing a lifetime in the physical Dimension, but you are not separated from your Soul, you are still your Soul, *and your Soul is Love !* and you begin to embrace that, you begin to show *Respect* for All other Beings on the Planet, because you are finally *respecting yourself !* Your Soul Dimension, we speak of it often, but it is not a single Dimension it is a multi Dimension, and there are wonders beyond belief waiting for you within those many Dimensions, let your judgements be based on the Love within your

Heart, and they will contribute to the quotient of Light upon the Earth Planet, instead of diminishing that Light and creating greater chaos and friction upon the Earth.

You often use the expression when something happens that goes wrong perhaps, and you say, "Ah, but I am only Human", as if that is something negative, Dear Hearts, it is *not*, being Human is something Glorious, for it is an opportunity to grow into your *Soul*, and to acknowledge and embrace the wondrous Being of Light that you are.

So in your Spiritual pursuits do not forget the physical representation of that, when you were a baby learning to crawl, learning to stand, learning to walk, the many bruises you suffered, but you came through, remember that. Dear Hearts, *You came through*, and you grew into what you are today, and now you are growing again, and you are learning again, growing and learning and *becoming the complete Light Being that you are*, not that you are meant to be, but that you *Are*.

You are taking the first steps, Dear Hearts, in becoming your Soul Incarnate, judge yourself lovingly, and you will judge others lovingly, and the essence of judging lovingly is ***Respect,*** respecting the beauty, respecting the authenticity of each and every other Being of Light upon the Earth Planet, embracing them, accepting them, For you are all One.

Dear Hearts, we thank you for allowing us to be with you again within this Sacred Space, and we ask you now to move deep into your Heart and embrace your journey into your ***Soul***.

(21ST November 2017)

23

WE ARE ALL ONE

(The Circle opens with the Sounds of the Tibetan Bowls and the drum)

Greetings, Dear Hearts, we are the Masters of Shambhala

Allow the Sound of the bowls and the drum to take you on a journey to the centre of your Being, to the place deep within your Heart that carries the Divine Light of your Soul, and allow yourself to move totally into your Soul Dimension, and take a moment to simply look upon your life from the frequency of the Soul Dimension, seeing yourself as an integral part of the whole, no longer an individual Being, but part of the One, and as you perceive yourself in this new Light, you see yourself as part of all upon the Earth, as part of the Earth itself, and you feel the power of the One, and your Consciousness is immediately expanded into Divine Light.

Take a moment to simply breathe in the energies of Oneness, and feel yourself releasing any strands of energy connecting you to anything that is not a part of that Oneness, releasing all the anchors to the old energy, to the old Dimension of duality and separation, and feel the power of freedom within yourself - for those in separation can never be free. It is only within the Oneness that freedom occurs.

Breathe in the energies of Freedom

Breathe in the energies of Love

Breathe in the energies of Peace

For as you breathe these energies into yourself, you breathe them into every Being upon the Earth - for as you empower your own Being, you empower all that are a part of the *One*.

This, Dear Hearts, is the true power of your Ascension, that as you breathe, as you Love, as you feel Peace, you are contributing to every other part of the whole, and you are allowing all those upon the Earth to be drawn deeper into their own Heart spaces, into their own Soul Dimensions, for those are ALL a part of the ONE.

On your Planet you are approaching that time which is known as the Wesak, embracing the energies of the Buddha. The Buddha came to the Earth to teach about Love and about Oneness, and has continued to teach those who are open to Love and Peace.

So, it is a powerful time upon your Planet for those who are Awakened to come together - to share their Love - *to BE the Oneness* - and *we*, as The Masters of Shambhala, will be waiting to embrace and empower each and every One of you within that Oneness, and we will breathe together the Love, the Peace, the Joy and the Harmony that the new Earth frequency requires.

So we invite you to participate in a celebration of the Wesak, to join us at Shambhala and contribute your wisdom that all may share the Love and the Light in a new Joyful celebration of *Oneness*.

We embrace you with deep Love, and we thank you for all the work you are doing to release the old energies of the Earth Planet, and to breathe your Love into the New Dimensional Frequencies of the Earth.

We are all One.

(15th April, 2013)

24

THE DARKNESS OF THE PAST WILL FADE INTO THE SUNSHINE OF TOMORROW

(The circle opens with the Sounds of the Tibetan bowls and the 'Cosmic Tone')

Feel the vibration of the Bowls, activating Joy throughout your Being, uplifting your Heart into the Soul Dimension, allowing you to become *One* with your Higher Vision, your Higher Perspectives, your Higher Frequencies of Light, and feel all the dross of the day falling away, enabling you to feel the True Lightness of your Being.

Breathe deeply of the Light within your Hearts, and allow that Light to radiate forth across the Earth Planet, enabling the Light Frequencies to rise up within *All* of Humanity. *Opening the doorway for each Being of Light to be uplifted into their own Soul Dimension.*

Greetings, Dear Hearts, We are the Masters of Shambhala,

We have come together once more to assist in the upliftment of the Earth Planet, and the upliftment of all upon and within the Earth Planet.

We are aware that for some time now many of you have felt lost, many of you have felt abandoned, but this is not so, you have been embraced constantly by the Love of the Creator, and you have been 'allowed' a period of time to find your feet in the new Dimensional Frequencies. You have been so accustomed to the old ways that it is not easy to let go, it is not easy to constantly look ahead and feel uplifted, for everything is different now, everything has changed within you, and upon the Earth.

It is like walking through a Forest that you have never seen before, your initial reaction is one of fear and trepidation, everything is unfamiliar. You cannot see ahead of you, merely a winding pathway through the trees, and some are holding back, wondering what is ahead. Some are racing forward eagerly, for they have accepted that what is ahead is Truth and Light, and they have no fear, they have only Love. But for the vast majority of Humanity there is this uncertainty and trepidation, and that is quite understandable, and you should not berate yourselves if this is how you have been feeling, give yourselves time to adjust to the *New Earth Frequencies,* give yourselves time to let go of the burdens of the past, give yourselves time to find the Love within your Hearts.

From time to time, we come together in Shambhala to provide a new Light Frequency for the Earth, and to plan how best we can assist Humanity in this monumental undertaking of Ascending themselves and the Earth as *One*, and we tend to use specific dates to introduce new Energies. because you have become so accustomed to your Calendar dates – you no longer work through the Planetary alignments as you once did.

So tonight we wish to alert you to the next inflow of *Divine Light,* on the 11th of the 11th, a date that we have worked with many times before, so we continue to work with that date. And we advise tonight that on that date – the 11th of the 11th – there will be an inflow of a new Frequency of Light that will uplift the Crystalline structures of the Earth into a New Harmonious Resonance, and because you too, as Humans, have undertaken the change to a Crystalline structure, you will be impacted quite dramatically by this inflow of Energy.

This Energy, this New Frequency of Light, will unlock the *"Pyramids of Joy"* all around the Earth, and the Energy of Joy will suffuse the whole Earth Planet, and of course, Humanity itself. You will begin to understand how to find true Joy within yourselves, how to perceive the world around you through the veil of Joy. As with the energy of Love, the Energy of Joy allows you to let go of fear, it allows you to see the world around you in a new and beautiful Light. You have an expression for this, *'looking at the world through Rose coloured spectacles', That is what will begin on the 11th of the 11th .*

You will look at areas of your Planet which in the past have given you great cause for concern, great pain, and emotional instability, and you will begin to see the seeds of Joy emerging from those areas. You will begin to see the other side of the coin, so to speak, rejecting the images of fear that are projected continuously though your media, and finding those seeds of Joy - and you will find those seeds growing deep within you, and you will begin to reach out to others with a new Energy, *an Energy of Joy.*

You have already found that many people have difficulty accepting the energy of Love that you transmit, you will find it much easier for people to accept the energy of Joy that you are 'offering', simply through being in their presence. As you become more joyful within yourself, that will flow out to others, *smiles* will become more prevalent, chasing away the shadows of fear and anger.

> *'Times they are a changing'*, it is up to each and every one of you how much of these changes you absorb into yourselves, how much of this *Energy of Joy* you take into yourself, and how much you change in your view of the world around you.

The *'Pyramids of Joy'* will be accessed and opened and their Energy, which has been stored upon this Planet of yours since the beginning of time, will permeate though every aspect of the Earth, you will see it in the creatures of the Earth, in the Plants of the Earth, each will have a new Energy, a new Aura that will bring a smile to your face, that is the

Energy of Joy, and as you smile, others will feel themselves drawn to smile also, and this ***will change the Energies of the Earth, totally, completely***

AND THE DARKNESS OF THE PAST WILL FADE INTO THE SUNSHINE OF TOMORROW.

(28TH October 2013)

25

WELCOME HOME, DEAR HEART, WELCOME HOME

(The circle opens with the Sound of the Tibetan bowls and the bells)

Embrace the vibrations and the Sound of the bowls and the bells, as they invite you to enter a new realm of Light, a new realm of Sound, a new realm of Higher Frequencies. Uplifting every part of your Being, calling to the deepest parts of your Heart, awakening every aspect of your Being to the energies of Love and Joy and Harmony.

Greetings, Dear Hearts, we are the Masters of Shambhala,

It is that time of your calendar year, the time approaching of the Solstice. And this is a time throughout millennia that Humanity has utilized as a focus point for the inflow of energies, for creating change upon your Earth, and this Solstice will be no exception, for we are radiating forth from Shambhala another Frequency of Light, at the time of your Solstice.

This is a Frequency of Light of HEALING, it is a Healing for all the Sacred Spaces of the Earth that have been abused and misused in the past, ***For it is a time of cleansing and healing the special places on the Earth Planet.*** Places like Avebury, Glastonbury, Stonehenge for those in the Northern Hemisphere, places which have been abused over many, many, many years, perceived as areas of darkness because they were gateways to other Dimensional Frequencies which were not understood by Humanity in those times. But as the Earth moves towards its Ascension these ***Power Sites*** need to be cleansed and Healed. So this will be the Frequency of Light that we will be sending to you at this next period of time, this next Solstice.

We invite you to embrace this energy within your Hearts and to allow yourselves to be cleansed and Healed of all the old energies of fear and discomfort in the face of other Dimensional Frequencies. As you have been on the Earth Planet many times you have accumulated these energies of fear, and it is time to let them go, to allow the energies of Oneness, of Harmony, of Love, of Joy, to once more come to the surface, to re-align the Gateways to other Dimensional Frequencies.

The Sacred Isle of Avalon cries out at this time for Healing, for an infusion of Love and Joy that will once again open the gates between the Dimensions, to allow a true understanding to emerge of the Wholeness of the Earth Planet, that there is no Inner Earth and surface Earth, ***ALL ARE ONE*** ! no longer separate, no longer divided, simply awaiting the Healing Light to once more open the gates.

There are many other areas of your Planet that we will be reaching out to Heal, to infuse with Light and Love, to enable Humanity to once again embrace the wholeness of the Earth, and to understand the wholeness of the Earth, and to embrace the Oneness with the Earth.

Over recent times, Dear Hearts, you have become increasingly aware that you exist in more than one Dimension, more than simply your Physical Beings, but many of you have yet to journey to the other Dimensions of yourselves, many of you still hold back, blinded by the Mists that have concealed the Gateways to other Dimensions for so long. With the new energy that we will be sending you on the Solstice these Mists will evaporate, and you will be *face to face with your own fears of the unknown*, but if you accept these energies into your own Hearts there will be no fear, there will be instead an *acceptance*, an *excitement* of discovery, discovering more about yourself, discovering more about your Earth, discovering more about *All that is.*

So we invite you, Dear Ones, at the time of your Solstice, to simply open your Hearts, consciously let go of the tendrils of fear that still hold you to the past, and to step forward to the Gateways between Dimensions and throw open the gates within yourself, and you will gain such Wisdom and such Knowing, that you will wonder why you have waited so long to *Find Yourself.*

The Bells and the Bowls are calling you, ringing out across the world *Calling you to find … YOU.*

It does not require any specific activity, any specific gathering, it simple requires you to begin the journey into yourself, completely free of fear, knowing with *absolute certainty* that you are Love. and Light, and

Joy. For the darkness is an illusion from the past that you have now let go, and the Mists will clear.

When the other Dimensional worlds open and embrace you, they will say to you

WELCOME HOME, DEAR HEART, WELCOME HOME

(16th December 2013)

26

PARIS CONFERENCE ON
CLIMATE CHANGE

(The Circle opens with the Sounds of the Tibetan bowls and the Blessings Chimes)

Perceive in your minds a magnificent crystal at the centre of this gathering radiating the Magenta Light out into the Hearts of all participants, allow Earth Mother to Love each and every one of these Beings into the Light of Possibilities.

Greetings, Dear Hearts, we are the Masters of Shambhala.

We have just a brief message for you tonight - a request if you like - for each one of you to move now deep into your Heart and empower the Love and the Light within your Heart and radiate it forth, for this is a powerful, perhaps even critical time on your

Planet, for as you know, Dear Hearts, the leaders of most of your countries are coming together in the city of Love that you called Paris, and *the purpose of this coming together is to determine what each and every one of them will do to assist the Planet Earth.*

It is never easy in gatherings of this nature for things to be achieved harmoniously, your press will no doubt focus on the differences that arise between different leaders, different countries and different vested interests, but we are asking you look upon this gathering as an opportunity to *focus more powerfully on the wellbeing of the Earth Planet than you have ever done before.*

Yes, Dear Hearts, there will be much talk about 'problems', because Humans tend to dwell on problems more than they dwell on possibilities, but if, Dear Hearts, Light Beings from all across the Planet focus the Love within their Hearts on this gathering in Paris without specific expectations of what will be achieved, perhaps the 'possibilities' will become more visible to those participating and the 'problems' less visible, for as we have often told you in other messages, what you focus upon is manifested - that is the manner of your Earth - *what*

you focus your attention on, what you focus your Love upon, what you focus your Hearts upon creates the world that will be.

You all know that efforts have already been made to cast a shadow over Paris, will you allow that to succeed ? or will you move back into your Hearts and focus your Love and your Light upon this gathering and empower the connection between those present within this gathering and the Magenta Light of Earth Mother? Ask for them all to be bathed by this Light, to have their Hearts opened to the *'essence' of Earth Mother,* and then allow them the space to grow with Earth Mother.

Yes, Dear Hearts, there have been similar gatherings before that have not succeeded, but that was the old energy, the energy before Earth Mother opened her Heart and cast out the Magenta Light into the Hearts of all upon the Planet, *this time, Dear Hearts, it will be different.*

This is a time of opportunity, a time of coming together in 'oneness of purpose'. We remind you, Dear Hearts, of recent messages that have said "do not look to blame others". It is all too easy within these gatherings and within those who surround these gatherings to start looking at who they can blame for all the problems that they perceive upon the Earth.

This is not a time for blame, Dear Hearts, this is a time for coming together with the possibilities of solution. So we come to you tonight and we say 'open your Hearts, flood the city of Love with the Love from within your Heart, join with Earth Mother to embrace each and every Heart within this gathering and allow the Magenta Light to take affect'.

Let go of blame, let go of judgments, reach out with your Heart, encircle this gathering of leaders of your Planet, nurture them with your Loving Light, let the past be the past, look to the future and allow the Love of Earth Mother, the Magenta Light from within her Heart, ***allow it, empower it, enable it*** to find a place within the Hearts of each of those participating in this gathering.

Embrace the Oneness of this gathering, perceive in your minds a magnificent crystal at the centre of this gathering radiating the Magenta Light out into the Hearts of all participants, ***allow Earth Mother***

to Love each and every one of these Beings into the Light of possibilities.

You may feel so far away, you can have no effect, but you know, Dear Hearts, you are all One and the energies you radiate forth will have an impact beyond anything your minds can imagine.

This is a special moment on your Planet; enable it to flower with the Magenta Light of Earth Mother and the Divine Love from within your Hearts.

Let that be your focus for the whole time that this gathering is taking place. Remember, Dear Hearts – no blame, no judgment, only Love, and in all your thoughts have Earth Mother at the centre of your Heart.

(30th November 2015)

27

YOU ARE ALWAYS RADIATING YOUR LIGHT

(The Circle opens with the Sounds of the Tibetan bowls and the Blessings Chimes.)

Greetings, Dear Hearts, we are the Masters of Shambhala.

We are delighted to be with you again tonight to share the Love and the Light within this Circle, to feel the embrace of your energies as you reach out from yourselves to embrace the Earth, to embrace the Cosmos, to be a special Light within the Universe, for indeed, Dear Hearts, the Universe is all about Light frequencies and Sound frequencies, and everything that exists is composed of both Light and Sound.

You yourselves are composed of Light and Sound, and there are times when you use that Sound to communicate your feelings, to communicate your Love, to others upon the Earth, there are other times when you simply focus your Light, and through that Light embrace others upon the Earth.

Those times when you are not speaking or utilizing your Sound Frequencies does not mean that you are not doing anything, you are always radiating your Light, your special Light, and that Light communicates as powerfully as any words or Sounds.

Sometimes what another person needs is a hug, an embrace, but other times they simply need to feel the warmth of your Light. ***So sit within your Hearts at all times and radiate forth your Light - your eternal Light -*** for the Light frequencies have nothing what so ever to do with your physical vessel, they are the essence of who and what you are, this combination of Light frequencies and Sound frequencies neither of which you may see with your Human eyes or hear with your Human ears, but that does not mean they do not exist. They are, and always will be the essence of who you are.

So simply focus on your Hearts, focus on the Love that is within your Hearts and allow that Love to be expressed through your Light and through your Sound. The Sound may be as soft as the beat of your Heart, and yet in that very softness is power, you reach out through your Heart, through the Sound of the beat of your Heart and you enlighten others, you bring joy to others.

Humans so often judge themselves against each other and feel inadequate, for Humans Love to feel inadequate. Sometimes it makes them try harder to be what they think others want them to be, but in reality you can only *BE* what you *ARE*, and it is your Light vibrations and your Sound vibrations that connect you to others, not how wise you are or how clever you are, but *the brightness with which you shine, and the Love with which you sound.*

You are moving into your season of goodwill, the time of the birth of the Christed energies into Humanity, a time when Light becomes important. It was the Light in the heavens that drew the three wise men to the birth of the Jesus.

Follow the Light within your Heart, just as the wise men did, they followed the Light within their Hearts and it brought them to the Christ Consciousness. No one needed to say anything, no one needed to do anything, they simply came to be with the Light.

You too, Dear Hearts, exist simply to draw others to your Light, for within your Light is your wisdom, and within your Sound is your Love. Gift both freely, let go of the doubts, let go of the judgments of self and simply

BE THE LIGHT AND THE SOUND OF "YOU".

(1st December 2014)

28

IT IS TIME TO LOOK AT YOUR WORLD, TO LOOK AT YOURSELVES, THROUGH YOUR HEART

(The Circle opens with the Sounds of the Tibetan bowls and the Blessings Chimes).

Allow yourselves to become aware of all the beautiful Light Beings that have gathered with you tonight and that are now sitting within your Hearts. Embrace their Light and their Love and feel the powerful energies of Oneness that you have now become, for within this Circle we are all connected, we are all a part of the whole - Human, Spirit, Cosmic, all within the beauty of your Heart.

Greetings, Dear Hearts, we are the Masters of Shambhala, and we welcome you into our Hearts as we sit within yours, and we feel the energy of Joy that is quickly becoming the essence of the Earth Planet.

We are most aware, Dear Hearts, that on the Earth Planet it is so easy to dismiss what you cannot see and often cannot feel, and to become disheartened and disappointed when your mind tells you that nothing is changing, that nothing is happening that has been promised to be happening. But that, Dear Hearts, is because you continue to look at your world through your Human eyes and through your logical minds, when as we have indicated to you before, *it is time to look at your world, to look at yourselves, through your Hearts, to see beyond the images that are projected within the lower dimensional frequencies that the Earth is gradually moving beyond.*

For example, Dear Hearts, many of you may feel that nothing has changed since the Earth opened its Heart at the time of the Solstice and poured forth the Magenta energies. You look around you and you see that life is very much the same, but I ask you, look again, look at what has happened in your world since the time of the Solstice, and yes, Dear Hearts, your mind will begin to twirl, and you will think "what is it that I am supposed to be looking at, the world is a vast and complex place, where should I be looking?".

Look at the traumas of your world, and ask yourselves "has that changed?" Indeed it has, Dear Hearts, I will give you but a small example – for many years there have been strife, problems, war, cruelties in the places you call Syria and Iraq and many hundreds of thousands of people have felt the need to flee, and for all this time they have sat in what you call refugee camps in adjoining countries, and no one has taken much notice. Oh yes, the world is aware that it is happening, but they have taken little notice, but since the Solstice, Dear Hearts, there has been a magnificent change and suddenly people are not sitting in their camps hidden from the world, there is suddenly a wave of people moving through countries, moving across Oceans and what is the result of that? - *Hearts are opening and embracing this wave of refugees.*

You see the Earth has opened its Heart, it has poured forth the Magenta energy of Love and Peace and it has begun to awaken the Compassion and the Love in Humans across the Planet. You are undoubtedly seeing vision of this on your television screens, but you are not seeing the underlying reality of the

Hearts opening to embrace those who are lost. Yes it is a tragedy that people are displaced from their homelands, but since the Solstice the energies have changed, people are reaching out to other people, and those other people are opening their Hearts and they are giving Love and Compassion like they have never given before.

So when you think to yourself "hmm, nothing really happened at the Solstice". I ask you to look again, to see the power and the influence that the Magenta Light from the Heart of Earth Mother is creating on your Planet.

Now, Dear Hearts, it is up to each and every one of you to become in some way involved in empowering that awakening, that embracing of Love for others, Compassion for others, for it is through this opening of the Heart, through the Love, through the Compassion, that the evil that has created the problem will be defeated, for you see, Dear Hearts, Love is at this time replacing fear and hatred.

The Solstice was much more powerful than you ever thought possible and that you have ever perceived since, and it is not going to go away, Dear Hearts, for in this coming month more beautiful electromagnetic energy will be pouring on to the Earth to further empower the Magenta Love and Peace, and Humanity will begin to realize that *the solution to most of the problems being created on this Planet at this time is Love – Unconditional Love*. This is what you are seeing in a small way at the moment as these waves of people march across Europe.

Oh yes, there are small pockets of people who are resenting this and who are trying to stop this, but overwhelmingly Hearts are opening to people they do not know. *THAT is unconditional, Dear Hearts, it is powerful, it is magical*, and as the new influx of electromagnetic energies from the Cosmos, from the centre of the Cosmos, from source itself comes to the Earth in coming weeks, you need to have your Hearts open, that those energies may empower the Unconditional Love within you and within the whole of humanity.

Dear Hearts, we do not try to tell you that everything will be magical, that every problem will be resolved with a click of the finger, *but look at what has begun*. Do not let your minds and your eyes dismiss what has happened, look beyond and see the upsurge of Love, the upsurge of opening Hearts and know that *this is indeed magical times for all upon the Earth Planet,* and we here in Shambhala are so uplifted by what we are seeing, and we too want to be a part of this upliftment, of this *Explosion of Love Energy.*

We will be with you, we will be working with you, prompting you, whispering in your ears as the weeks go by, bringing to your awareness that which you cannot yet see because *the vision is not for the Human eyes, it is for the Human Heart.*

You may look at your television screens and feel saddened by what you are seeing, you should be feeling joyful about what you are seeing, for Love, Caring and Compassion are flowering right across the Earth, empowered and emboldened by the beautiful Magenta Energy from the Heart of Earth Mother.

Be prepared, Dear Hearts, for a major inflow of energy that will further empower the Magenta Love from Earth Mother.

> *This is the beginning of a new age of Compassion and Love on your Earth.*

(7th September 2015)

29

YOU ARE EACH A DIAMOND OF LIGHT IN THE CROWN OF THE COSMOS

(The Circle opens with the Sounds of the Tibetan Bowls).

Feel the resonance of the Tibetan Bowls radiating through every aspect of your Being, shifting all the shadows within you and bringing them into the Light of Divine Love, and feel yourself being uplifted into a new frequency of Light, of Love, of Sound.

Allow your Hearts to embrace the energies of the Bowls, and feel that energy flowing out from your Heart across the Earth Planet, creating the Divine Sound and Light of Healing for all those in need of healing tonight.

Greetings Dear Hearts. We are the Masters of Shambhala.

We reach out and embrace you and invite you to join us in Shambhala, lifting the energies of your Heart, into the Heart of your Soul, and finding yourself sitting with us in Shambhala, for we have marveled at the immense Light and Love that has burst from the Earth Planet since the Equinox.

Yes, we have gathered together once more that we may look afresh at what is happening upon the Earth, and through the Earth into the Cosmos, for the Light and Love that you have created upon your Planet goes far beyond the limitations of your Planet, and flows out into the Universe singing joyfully of upliftment, of Light, of Love.

You have far surpassed the expectations of all of us, and we honor you for the work that you have done, and the work that you continue to do.

Each one of you is powerful beyond measure, but together you are undefeatable, you are Pure Light, you are Divine Love, and we ask to share those energies with you now.

The time of perceiving the Masters as being remote from you is over, for *you have joined the Circle of Masters at Shambhala.* All of you within this Circle, and all of you around the Planet who came together at the Equinox, have come together now to share Divine Love, Divine Light, and to feel the power of working in Unity.

Take a moment to allow your energies to adjust to ours. Do so knowing you are equal, that you are a part of all that is, that *you are each a diamond of Light in the crown of the Cosmos.*

From time to time, we have spoken to you of discernment, and we wish to address momentarily that subject once again, for it is important to recognize that discernment is not judgment. Discernment is simply an acceptance of what is appropriate for you.

You receive messages from many sources. Discernment is accepting those messages which uplift, which enhance your Light, and letting go of those that do not. When you let go of those that do not enhance your own Light, do not do so with the assumption that those messages are somehow flawed or wrong. Know that they will be appropriate for others on the journey to Ascension.

147

There is no judgment in letting go of those messages that are not for you. Simply accept that somewhere, someone will be enlightened by the words within those messages, and honour all the wisdom that you receive.

It is important that you recognize discernment as an acceptance, and not a judgment.

There are many changes taking place on the Earth at this time, and with changes comes confusion and seeming chaos, and Humanity throughout its history has often reacted to these changes by pulling up the drawbridge, battening down the hatches, and waiting it out.

That may have been appropriate, Dear Hearts, when the changes were outside, but these changes, Dear Ones, are all within you, and if you pull up the drawbridge and batten down the hatches, you will simply stifle the flow of energy from these changes, and in so doing you may create distortion within yourself.

Dear Hearts, throw away your hatches, let down the drawbridge, and let the energies of change from within yourself radiate outwards into the Earth, for it is only when you accept the flow of energy, that change becomes meaningful for the Earth Planet.

Energy must flow freely. It is not owned by any one individual, any more than wisdom is owned by any one individual. It is a flow, a flow of energy.

Be part of that flow, give of your Light, give of your Wisdom, **share**, share at all times, and in so doing you will see that you are influencing the changes around you.

You have received messages today, about changing, about allowing, about embracing the energies of the time, and we ask you to do this, to become part of the flow of Light as you did at the Equinox.

If you could have seen the explosion of Light from the Earth at that time, you would be in awe, but then in part you did – *for you were given pictures that reflected the explosion of Light that moved from your Hearts, and moved from your Circle, out into the world, and out into the Cosmos*. You were part of the flow of Light, and the flow of Love.

Remember always to allow yourself to be a part of that flow, always with the highest good in your Heart, looking at your journey ahead through the

Heart of your Soul, and knowing that All will be - for all is possible.

We invite you to take your time and simply **BE** a part of the energy of Shambhala, and we embrace you with such Love and such Light, and we honor you.

And so it is.

(8th October 2012)

30

OPEN YOURSELF TO THE
ENERGY OF ONENESS

(The Circle opens with the Sounds of the Tibetan Bowls)

Relax and allow the vibrations of Sound to lift you up into the essence of your Divine Soul, feeling the vibrations of Bliss taking form within your physical body, enabling each aspect of your Being to be raised in vibration, to feel totally uplifted as if on a cloud.

And, as you allow yourselves to be uplifted in vibration, you open the gateways to connection with other Beings of Light, in other Dimensions, and we stand within those gates welcoming you, embracing you with Deepest Love.

We greet you, Dear Ones, we are the Masters of Shambhala, and it is with great joy that we entertain you this evening, and embrace the Light that you are creating within yourselves for the upliftment of the Earth Planet itself.

'Introspection' has been the key word for this period since the Great Shift. We have invited you to move deep within yourselves, and embrace those aspects of self that will assist you in the vibrational frequency of the New Earth, and invited you to let go of all aspects that no longer resonate with the new vibrational frequencies.

And you have done this in different ways, at different times, and the majority of you have found that Inner Peace deep within yourselves, and you have made space within yourselves to embrace the new realities of the New Dimensional frequencies of the Earth and of yourselves.

Introspection sometimes creates a belief within you that you are standing still, but we are here to tell you that you have not been standing still, for as you have released baggage from the past, you have increased the pace at which you move towards your New Light Beingness, sometimes like a balloon moving up into the sky, dropping the weights that held it down, increasing its speed, and yet when you are within that balloon, it does not feel as if you are moving at all.

But now, Dear Ones, the time for introspection is coming to an end. As you approach that time you call the Equinox, there will be a great infusion of Cosmic energy into the Earth, and the real journey for each of you will begin in earnest. The introspection has been a preparation for the next magnificent step of your journey.

This particular Circle has worked with the Equinox for a considerable time, so you will have no problems in focusing at that time, in embracing the changes that will happen at that time.

In the past you have focused upon your Oceans, the 'Consciousness of your Oceans', for it was necessary to alert others around your Planet to the existence of the Consciousness of the Oceans of the Earth, and you may wonder why it is no longer necessary for you to do this, and the answer to that, Dear Ones, is quite simple.

You have moved into the Dimension of Oneness, and the Ocean Consciousness is no longer separate from the Consciousness of Humanity. You are all now ONE, so there is no need to alert others around the Planet to the existence of something which is already now within themselves.

So the focus at the time of this Equinox will not be on the Consciousness of the Oceans:

It will be on the *Oneness of all that is*.

It will be on the *interconnectedness of all Beings upon and within the Earth.*

It will be the beginning of a New Brotherhood of Healing.

Beloved Germain spoke of the Brotherhood of Healing when he gifted you the Marine Meditation so many years ago. Now this will become a reality, Energetically, Spiritually, but because this will be happening energetically, it will gradually filter down into the physical, and you will see many substantial changes around your world, changes at high levels, and these changes will have profound significance for the future of the Earth.

The Masters of Shambhala have come together yet again in preparation for the Equinox, to bring to bear upon the Earth the fullness of the power of your Spiritual friends, to ensure that the changes take place with ease and grace upon your Earth.

Many, many more Beings will awaken in the months to come. Many more who will not necessarily be awakened will begin to see things differently, will begin to question the fabric of authority, and when I speak of authority, I speak of course of those who seek to control others - and they will question, and *the power will fade from those who are not of the Light.*

For within the Dimension of Oneness there will be no room for the shadows of the past. Every Being who has agreed to be on the Earth Planet at this time will take on board more and more Light, and will become more and more Loving in their interaction with others.

Now, Dear Ones, we do not pretend this is going to happen all in one day, that suddenly on the Equinox everyone will love everyone. It is a slow process, but it is already well in train. You have contributed much over many years to bring this about at this time.

So as you approach this Equinox, open yourself to the Energies of Oneness. Let go of judgement, open your arms and embrace your fellow Beings on the Planet with your Energy of Love, for it is the Energy of Love that will create the changes on your Planet.

We invite you to sit awhile with us here at Shambhala, and allow the Energies of Love that exist here to fill you, that you may share these energies with all those around you on the Earth Planet.

> *__Feel__ the Oneness.*
> *__Know__ the Oneness.*
> *For Oneness is the new reality.*
> *It dispels all illusions.*
> *__Love is the power.__*
> *__Love is all.__*

(11ᵗʰ March 2013)

31

IT IS WITHIN YOUR SOUL DIMENSION THAT YOU WILL GAIN THE GREATER UNDERSTANDING OF THE JOURNEY THAT YOU ARE ON

(The Circle opens with the Sounds of the Tibetan Bowls)

Feel the bowls uplifting your spirits, moving you upwards into your Soul Dimension, allowing you to have an oversight of your lives at this time.

Greetings Dear Hearts, we are the Masters of Shambhala.

This one (*David*) thought he would get away with it tonight, but that is not to be so - (*chuckle*). We have come together once more at this time of the Lions Gate, to work with the powerful energies of the

Cosmos that are flowing into the Earth at this time, ***energies of Divine Love.***

We have spoken to you often about the importance of Love as an energy rather than as a Human emotion, but of course as energies of Love come into the Earth Planet more powerfully, these will attach themselves to a degree to your emotions, and you may find yourselves less balanced emotionally than you normally are. At those times it is important that you allow yourselves to be uplifted into your Soul Dimension.

Imagine yourself simply getting into a lift (*elevator*) and moving upwards into your Soul Dimension, and as the lift (*elevator*) doors open you step out onto your Soul Dimension and you look afresh at your journey, at the Earth, at the energies surrounding the Earth, and you will find yourself immediately re - balanced, for you will no longer be locked into the emotions of the moment, you will no longer be confined within the parameters of the old Earth, you will see and feel the energies of Divine Love flowing powerfully to, through, and around you, and the Earth.

You will feel totally balanced and yet uplifted and excited by the visions before you. For the energies of Divine Love encourage, enlightenment, upliftment and excitement at every level of your Being.

For this is not a time to be anchoring into the Earth. It is a time to be anchoring into your Soul Dimension, for as you anchor into your Soul Dimension you lift the Earth Planet with you into that higher frequency, so by anchoring yourself at the higher frequency levels you are assisting the Earth to be uplifted also.

Think about that for a moment, Dear Ones - It is not a time to be holding yourselves back by anchoring downwards, it is now in the best interests of yourselves and of the Earth Planet to be anchoring upwards into the Soul Dimension, which acknowledges and accepts the Oneness of all that is.

You see, anchoring downwards
is motivated by fear.
Anchoring upwards is motivated by Love.

The balance you achieve in your Soul Dimension is the balance that is needed in the new Earth frequencies, and we at Shambhala seek to encourage you to be uplifted at all times, to be ever looking upwards. The energies flowing through the Lions Gate at this time are designed to be uplifting.

Feel those energies now flowing through your bodies, filling your Heart, and feel yourselves becoming lighter and lighter, allowing you to move with greater purpose upwards into your Soul Dimension, for it is within your Soul Dimension that you will gain the greater understanding of the journey that you are on, and the journey that the Earth Planet is on at this time, and in that understanding you will find a clarity, a vision, a new Light along your pathway.

Dear Hearts, do not worry that by anchoring into the Soul Dimension you will lose your connection to the Earth Planet, this is not so, you will lift the Earth Planet with you into the Higher Dimensional Frequencies, for you are ONE with the Earth.

We will continue to work with you to achieve the goals that you have set for your own Ascension and the Ascension of the Earth, for *We are also One with YOU.*

We bless you and we thank you.

(12th August 2013)

32

ONE WAVE OF LIGHTWORKERS IS COMING TO AN END, AND ANOTHER WAVE IS JUST BEGINNING

(The gathering opens with the Sounds of the Tibetan Bowl, the Drum and the Peace and Harmony Chimes)

Greetings, Dear Hearts, we are the Masters of Shambhala

We are aware that you have been waiting patiently for some time to hear from us, and we apologize for the delay in communicating with you at this time, but the gathering at Wesak went for much longer than we had anticipated, for a whole variety of reasons.

Our Gathering on this occasion was addressed by Beloved Earth Mother, as well as by Beloved Tarak and Beloved Margot, all of whom confirmed that the **new Arcturian Peace Energy** which was shared with the Earth Planet between your Equinox and your Solstice had indeed been firmly embedded within the Songlines of the Earth Planet and within the Crystalline Grid System itself, and had been aligned fully with the Consciousness of the Peace Energy that had been transmitted through Mount Kailash.

Now, Dear Hearts, this had not been an easy task, and there had been considerable disruption upon the Earth Planet, both within the Earth itself and also with those **'Sensitives'** amongst Humanity that were attuned to this process. This is a time upon the Earth Planet of great change, and as with all change, there is a period of turbulence – Beloved Germain referred to it as **'Turmoil'** – during which it is difficult to see the Light at the end of the tunnel. But we assure you, Dear Hearts, there is considerable Light at the end of the tunnel.

But part of the changes that are taking place, particularly amongst Humanity, is that one wave of Light Workers is coming to an end, and another wave is just beginning. I am sure that you will have noticed over the past year of your linear time that many of our messengers have either departed the Earth Planet or have drawn back into relative silent contemplation of their own, and the messages that were being transmitted to Humanity through these beautiful people have been less frequent than before. This is not because your Spiritual and Cosmic friends have deserted you, Dear Hearts, it is simply a part of the process of change, as the Wayshowers of this generation move on, new Wayshowers appear, bringing with them New Wisdom, New Knowledge, New Joy, and New Love. But it *IS* a difficult time of transition, and we ask you to bear with us at this time, as these changes are taking place.

Do not bemoan the loss of the Wayshowers of the past, instead, embrace the Light of Wayshowing within yourself !, for indeed, Dear Hearts, in this *'New Age'* this *'New Time'* the Secret – if there is such a thing as a Secret – is for each and every one of you to move into your own Hearts and open up to the Wisdom within yourselves. We are sure, Dear Hearts, that if you go back over the messages of the last few years, you will see a pattern where each one of you are being urged to look within your own Hearts. Yes, Dear Hearts, it is important to share, it is important to listen to others, for each person's knowledge and Wisdom is different.

It is time to stop living in a single bubble of 'belief system' and to open yourself to the Oneness of all that is.

Beloved Earth Mother has been delighted with the amount of *Light* upon the Earth as more and more Hearts awaken to the Truth of themselves, to the truth of Earth and to the Truth of the Cosmos.

Much Light is being shed upon dark areas of the past, and you are all being invited to ***BE IN JOY WITHIN YOUR HEARTS***, for the more you reside in Joy, the greater your Light will be, and the greater the *Light* you share, the greater the number of people awakening will be.

It is time now to move to a new stage of Earth's Journey, a stage of constant ***EN – LIGHTEN – MENT.*** It is a time to come together more frequently and, perhaps, in greater numbers, for when you join together you create greater and greater *Light* upon the Earth, and you speed up the evolution and the journey towards ultimate Ascension of the Earth Planet.

And now, Dear Hearts, you are coming to the time that you know as the ***Lion's Gate***, a time of connection and communication, particularly with the Beings of Sirius. Now as you know, Dear Hearts, the Beings that work constantly to balance and Harmonize the 12 Songlines of this Planet, Dylanthia and Arrantha are Sirians, so we ask you now to focus upon Sundown Hill and Dylanthia, and send your love to her, to enable her to continue to work for the Earth Planet. I speak now only of Broken Hill for the time, for I am coming through this one who is living within Australia, but it equally applies to Arrantha, give her your Love also at Machu Picchu.

The essence on this occasion of the greater connection through the ***Lion's gate*** continues to be the inflow of the ***Arcturian Peace Energies***, for nothing happens in a short space of time in your Linear time, it is an ongoing process that requires each and every one of you to participate on a daily basis, by opening your Hearts, sending your Love through the Songlines of the Earth Planet, and embracing Earth Mother at every opportunity.

Dear Hearts, we are all in this together, do not be saddened should you lose more of your Wayshowers in the coming times, for they will be moving on to assist the Earth in other Dimensional frequencies. The legacy that they will leave behind is an inexorable movement towards Ascension, towards greater and greater *Light* upon the Earth Planet, and this is something to be Joyful about.

Dear Hearts, we will meet again shortly, but for now we simply ask you all to focus on the *Lion's gate* on the day that you call the 8th of the 8th and embrace the Light and the Love of the Beings of Sirius, who come each year to offer you *Love, Light, Joy and Peace*.

Blessings be with you.

(13th July 2017)

33

EMPOWER THE ENERGIES OF LOVE WITH EVERY BREATH YOU TAKE

(The Circle opens with the Sounds of the Tibetan Bowls and the Bell)

Allow the waves of Sound to permeate every aspect of your Being, uplifting you into the realms of Light and Love and Joy. Feel yourself becoming alive in a new and glorious way as every part of your physical body vibrates with the new frequency of Love, a Love that is all encompassing, totally fulfilling, then allow that vibration of Love to radiate forth from your Being, reaching out to every corner of your Earth, singing the Heart Song of Love, of Harmony, of Joy, of Peace.

For many around the world at this time are sorely in need of these energies as they waken to the darkness surrounding them. They are ready to receive the

Light and the Love, the Harmony and the Peace to uplift them so allow the Love within your Heart to move out across the Earth on the vibrations of Sound.

Greetings, Dear Hearts, we are the Masters of Shambhala.

We are together once more in Shambhala to decide and determine the next steps in the Ascension of the Earth Planet and all upon it, not because we, as a Council, direct that Ascension, we are merely here to assist you and all the other Beings of Light upon the Earth Planet to find the most appropriate ways that you can assist in your own Ascension and in the Ascension of the Earth Planet itself.

You will be well aware that there are number of Planetary alignments this month, a Cardinal Cross, a Lunar Eclipse, all these, Dear Hearts, provide gateways to other Dimensional frequencies, and we invite you to step through those gateways to other Dimensional frequencies, and to draw from those other Dimensions the necessary energies to assist you in your own upliftment, and to empower you to share that upliftment with others.

As you know, Dear Hearts, in your cultures the moon is regarded as the emotion, and an eclipse of the moon is a clearing of the emotional dis-harmonies within the Planet, so you are invited to take this special time of your Lunar Eclipse to wash away any dis-harmonious energies that you may be holding onto in your life, to release yourself from emotional ties to the past. *It is a cleansing of emotional energies.*

The alignments of other Planets will bring different energies to the Earth, and you need to be sensitive to how those energies relate to you, and react with you, for this is a communal Ascension process. *There is the individual that is you, and there is the Oneness that is the whole.* Both need to be in alignment at this time, to access and magnify the energies being created by these Planetary alignments.

You may look around your World at this time and see aspects that you do not resonate with. Do not judge them, Dear Hearts, simply embrace them with all the Love that is within your Hearts, allowing each and every one upon the Planet to find within themselves the Love and the Light that is necessary for their Ascension, neither you nor we can command the changes, we can only participate in the changes, with intent, and that intent is pure Love – Love of self, Love of all – pure Love.

We suggest, Dear Hearts, that you take some time in the weeks to come to move into the stillness of your Heart, and radiate forth the Love that is there. Empower with every breath you take, the energies of Love.

You are, of course, approaching that time in your Christian calendar, the time of change, of death and rebirth, of renewal of the Christ energies. Again, Dear Hearts, do not look at the illusions that your religions have created, look through the window, through the gateway of the Christ energies, and embrace the pure Love that is embodied in that time.

It is indeed, Dear Hearts, a time of renewal, not necessarily as dramatic as the religions would have you believe, but it is a time of renewal, a time of letting go of the old, the old body, the old ideals and then when you have spent some time in the stillness of your Hearts, to rebirth your commitment to the upliftment of the Earth and the Ascension of your own Being.

Look deep within yourselves, find the Love, the Light, the Joy, the Harmony and, <u>most of all</u>, the Peace, and share that with all those around you, not judging, not crying out for specific reactions from them, but simply embracing them with the deepest Love in your Heart and sharing all that is YOU.

(14th April 2014)

GLOSSARY

Ascended Masters - Spiritually Enlightened Beings who have previously incarnated in Human form on the Earth but who are now in Higher Dimensional Frequencies.

Wesak – A celebration of the Birth, Enlightenment and Ascension of the Buddha.

Shambhala - A 'City of Light' in Higher Dimensional frequencies where Spiritual and Cosmic Beings work together in Oneness. Some perceive it to be situated Energetically above the Wesak Valley in Tibet. Channeled information given to me indicates that Shambhala is a structure within the Etheric comprised of 6 energy Pyramids of the 4 sided variety, connected together to form the Sacred Geometric shape of a Merkaba.

Pendragon – When David J Adams moved house in 2006 he was told in a dream that the House would be called 'Pendragon', so from that time his Meditation Circle became known as Pendragon Meditation Circle. Pendragon, of course, was the Name given to Welsh Kings of old like Uther Pendragon (father of Arthur of the Round Table), so could be a reflection of David's Welsh heritage.

Songlines – there are 12 major songlines throughout the Earth which come together at two places, Sundown Hill just outside Broken Hill in Australia (they are represented here by Sculptures) and Machu Picchu in Peru. They are vibrational, or Sound Arteries of the Planet.

Willow Springs – Willow Springs Station is situated in the Flinders Ranges of South Australia and is a Sacred Space within which lies a confluence of the Michael and Mary Lines similar to that which exists beneath Glastonbury Tor in the UK. The two sites are energetically linked. (*See following Article*)

Sundown Hill - Sundown Hill is situated just outside Broken Hill in New South Wales, Australia. There are 12 large Sculptures on the top of the Hill created by artists from many parts of the World. As we understand it, these Sculptures mark one of the two confluences of the 12 Songlines of the Earth Planet, the other being Machu Picchu in Peru.

Blessings Chimes – A hand held instrument created from wind Chimes which are used to Bless the Earth, the Oceans and all Beings of Light upon the Earth.

Crystalline Grid – A structured network of Crystals throughout the Earth that are part of the electromagnetic composition of the Earth.

Isle of Avalon – A sacred Site at Glastonbury in the United Kingdom. The Glastonbury Tor is the remnant of this Island that housed the Divine Feminine aspects of the 'old Earth' religions. It continues to exist, but in another Dimensional form and is a 'gateway' to other Dimensions. It is also regarded as the **HEART CHAKRA** of the Earth Planet.

Equinox - An **equinox** is commonly regarded as the moment when the plane of Earth's equator passes through the center of the Sun's disk, which occurs twice each year, around 20 March and 23 September. In other words, it is the point in which the center of the visible sun is directly over the equator.

Solstice - A **solstice** is an event occurring when the Sun appears to reach its most northerly or southerly excursion relative to the celestial equator on the celestial sphere. Two solstices occur annually, on about 21 June and 21 December. The seasons of the year are directly connected to both the solstices and the equinoxes.

Marine Meditation – This was a Global Meditation initiated by Beloved Germain to be held at 8pm on each Equinox, wherever people were in the world. It focused on connecting with the **CONSCIOUSNESS OF THE OCEANS**. It ran from March 1991 to September 2012 - 22 years and 44 meditations in all. See http://www.dolphinempowerment.com/MarineMeditation.htm

Dr Emoto - Masaru Emoto was a Japanese author, researcher, photographer and entrepreneur, who studied the Consciousness of Water, and showed through his photography that sound and words create changes in water molecular structure.

Mount Kailash – Mount Kailash is a peak in the Kailash Range in Tibet. Mount Kailash is considered to be Sacred in four Religions, Buddhism, Hinduism, Bon and Jainism.

Lion's Gate - Every year on August 8th, there is a cosmic alignment called "the Lions Gate". The Lions Gate is when Earth aligns with the Galactic Center, (27 degrees Sagittarius) and the star Sirius, opening a cosmic portal between the physical and spiritual realms.

Labyrinth: A Sacred Geometric Design or Pattern that creates a Path or journey to the center, and a return along the same route. On a Spiritual level it represents a metaphor for the journey to the centre of your deepest self, and back out into the world with a broadened understanding of who you are. With a Labyrinth there is only one choice to make, that choice is to enter or not, that choice is to walk the Spiritual path in front of you, or not. The choice is always yours to make within your Heart. There is no right or wrong way to walk a Labyrinth, you only have to enter and follow the path to the Center – the Center of yourself. Walk it in **LOVE**, walk it in **PEACE** and walk it in **RESPECT.**

Labyrinth of Inner Vision: (Front Cover Picture) The Labyrinth is comprised of 5 'Stations' joined by Tubes, or 'Tunnels of Light'. Each 'Station' represents a 'Dimensional Portal'. The first 'Station' is the 5th Dimensional Frequency and is represented visually by a circle containing a Heart overlaid by a Peace Symbol. You move through the 'Tunnel of Light' to the next 'Station' representing the 6th Dimensional Frequency, this is the Frequency of **'AWAKENING'**, and is represented visually by a circle containing a rising Sun, a new dawn for Humanity and the Earth. You move through the 'Tunnel of Light' to the next 'Station' representing the 7th Dimensional Frequency, this is the Frequency of **'TRANSFORMATION'**, the movement into 'Knowing' and 'Understanding', and is represented by a circle containing a Butterfly. You then move through the 'Tunnel of Light' to the next 'Station' representing the 8th Dimensional Frequency, this is the Frequency of **'ENLIGHTENMENT'** or **'ILLUMINATION'**, and is represented visually by a circle containing a White Candle shedding its Light to cast away the darkness of 'Fear' and 'Ignorance'. Finally you move through the 'Tunnel of Light' to the Heart of the Labyrinth, to the 'Station' representing the 9th Dimensional Frequency, this is the Frequency of **'INNER VISION'**, and is represented visually by a circle containing the 'Eye of Horus', enabling one to **'SEE ALL'** within and without one's own **BEING**. The Labyrinth of Inner Vision holds the Harmonic note of **EAGLE**.

We are all ONE: Back cover Lyrics are from the song "We are all ONE" written, performed and recorded by David J Adams, which can be heard and downloaded free of charge at **https://soundcloud. com/david-j-adams/03-we-are-all-one**

SONGLINES - NAMES AND APPROXIMATE ROUTES

We have given names to the 12 Songlines that embrace the Earth Planet based on the names of the 12 Sculpture on Sundown Hill, just outside Broken Hill in New South Wales, Australia. Below we give the approximate routes that the Songlines take between Sundown Hill and Machu Picchu as they were given to us in meditation.

RAINBOW SERPENT: Sundown Hill – Willow Springs – Mount Gee (Arkaroola) – Kings Canyon (near Uluru) – Mount Kailash (Tibet) – Russia – North Pole – via the North American Spine to Machu Picchu.

MOTHERHOOD: Sundown Hill – India – South Africa – follows the Nile River to North Africa – Machu Picchu.

181

THE BRIDE: Sundown Hill – Pacific Rim of Fire – Machu Picchu.

MOON GODDESS: Sundown Hill – Across the Nullabor to Perth – Madagascar – Mount Kilimanjaro – Egypt (Hathor Temple) – Via the Mary Line to the United Kingdom – Machu Picchu.

BAJA EL SOL JAGUAR (UNDER THE JAGUAR SUN): Sundown Hill – Grose Valley (New South Wales) – New Zealand – Chile – Via the Spine of South America (Andes) – Machu Picchu.

ANGELS OF SUN AND MOON: Sundown Hill – Willow Springs - Curramulka (Yorke Peninsular of South Australia) – Edithburgh (also Yorke Peninsular of South Australia) - Kangaroo Island – Mount Gambier - Tasmania – South Pole - Machu Picchu.

A PRESENT TO FRED HOLLOWS IN THE AFTERLIFE: Sundown Hill – Arltunga (Central Australia) – Through the Gold Light Crystal to Brazil – along the Amazon to Machu Picchu.

TIWI TOTEMS: Sundown Hill – South Sea Islands – Hawaii – Mount Shasta (USA) – Lake

Moraine (Canada) – via Eastern Seaboard of USA to Machu Picchu.

HORSE: Sundown Hill – Philippines – China – Mongolia – Tibet – Europe – France – Machu Picchu.

FACING THE NIGHT AND DAY: Sundown Hill – Queensland (Australia) – New Guinea – Japan – North Russia to Finland – Sweden – Norway – Iceland – Tip of Greenland – Machu Picchu.

HABITAT: Sundown Hill via Inner Earth to Machu Picchu.

THOMASINA (JILARRUWI – THE IBIS): Tension Lynch pin between Sundown Hill and Machu Picchu.

WILLOW SPRINGS

Willow Springs is a 'Station' (a little like a ranch in the USA) in the Flinders Ranges of South Australia, approximately 470km (or 5 and a half hours) north of Adelaide.

How we came to be connected to the Sacred Space on this property is explained below.

Back on 21 October 1998. Harmonic and Earth Walker, Krista Sonnen and her friend Sjoerd Tyssen (an incarnate Arcturian) set out on a bush walking trip to the Flinders Ranges, and had been told of a place called Willow Springs to stay

She and David J Adams had a last channeling session on the morning they were leaving. During the session they were asked to create an 8 pointed star Medicine Wheel there, which David subsequently drew a picture of.

On arrival at Willow Springs they approached the owners with the rather strange request to lay out a Medicine Wheel on the property, and they kindly agreed even though both were surely mystified by our explanations. They eventually found a flat and open enough spot to lay out the Medicine Wheel, with small stones lying abundantly around the area. When the Medicine Wheel was completed, it was honoured in ceremony.

On their return from Willow Springs, in another channeling session with David, Krista was told that they had been guided to lay out the Medicine Wheel at a confluence point of the Michael and Mary lines - Referred to as 'Rivers of energy'.

Curious about this, Krista contacted a friend who was an eminent South Australian Dowser and Earth Energies worker, and asked if he could map dowse the area to see if this information was correct. Not having a sufficiently detailed map of the area he was unable to do that, however, some 6 months later he was physically in the Flinders Ranges and remembered the request, and when he saw a sign post to Willow Springs he diverted from his route to check things out.

He was quite astonished at the results of his dowsing, for not only was the Michael and Mary confluence precisely where Krista had told him, but the Medicine Wheel itself was in perfect alignment with both the Curry and the Hartmann grids. He wrote up all this information, with diagrams, for the April 1999 edition of the SA Dowsers Newsletter.

We have learned from many of our Beloved "Spirit" companions that the Medicine Wheel connects us to Lemuria, to the Arcturus star system and beyond, and that it is also a meeting place of the Indigenous Spirit Elders Council of this area of Australia

Now, alongside the Medicine Wheel we have been advised that there is an Etheric Pyramid of Sound, accessed through a Rainbow Doorway. This Sound Pyramid is now the workplace of a beautiful Arcturian Sound Master called Tarak, as well as many Harmonic Beings, and if you stand within the Medicine Wheel and connect to the Sound Pyramid you can ask for … and receive … blessings, as well as giving out your blessings through them. Whenever you are within the Medicine Wheel there is always an exchange of energies happening if you have an OPEN HEART.

Various other 'Etheric' structures have been brought to our attention or have been laid out by subsequent visitors to Willow Springs. and one is a significant and powerful energy coming from a double terminated Etheric Crystal gifted to the area by our Arcturian friends. It sits with one point in the earth itself and the other above the earth and spins. The spinning motion radiates the LOVE and WISDOM of the Arcturians over a vast area. The Crystal itself has a huge circumference of approximately 10 kilometers, so it's energy spread is immense, added to this is the fact that it connects to at least three other Arcturian Etheric Crystals gifted to the Earth Planet in recent years. So be aware that you are dealing with powerful Cosmic energies. Focus on the JOY that is the Lighted Journey ahead.

Beloved Tarak, Sound Master of Arcturus, has based his Earth Healing and Sounding work from the Etheric Pyramid of Sound, which sits on the Rainbow Serpent Songline, so he can work powerfully with the Songlines of the Earth.

Please Note: As Willow Springs is a private property, please call the owners beforc accessing the property.

http://www.skytrekwillowsprings.com.au/

HOW TO MAKE YOUR OWN
BLESSINGS CHIMES

Blessings Chimes have a triangular wooden top. Inserted into the underside of the wooden triangle are a series of Screw Eyes with a series of chimes dangling from them with THREE 'Strikers' of your own design. The chimes are of different sizes, thicknesses or metals to provide a variety of Tones (which we created by taking apart a number of different, inexpensive, wind chimes). The Screw Eyes are set out in 5 rows from which the Chimes are hung, a single chime at the tip of the triangle, then 2 chimes, then 3 chimes, then 5 chimes and finally 7 chimes. This makes 18 chimes in all. One Screw Eye from which a 'Striker' hangs is placed between rows 2 and 3, and then two Screw Eyes from which 'Strikers' hang are placed between rows 4 and 5.

The 'Strikers' used in creating our Original Blessings Chime for the Marine Meditation had as decorations a Sea horse, a Unicorn, and a Dragon. The Triangular wooden top has a small knob on it, to hold as you shake the Blessings Chimes to create the vibration and resonance.

Although the original has a triangular Top and 18 chimes, you can vary this to your own intuition. The latest version that has been created for David has an Octagonal top and only 8 chimes and is called 'Peace and Harmony Chimes' rather than 'Blessings Chimes' to reflect it's more subtle Sound. Use your imagination and Intuition.

Blessings of Love and Peace

David J Adams